A Diver's Guide to

THE ART
OF UNDERWATER
PHOTOGRAPHY

Andrea & Antonella Ferrari

A Diver's Guide to

THE ART OF UNDERWATER PHOTOGRAPHY

NAUTILUS
publishing

The authors wish to express their gratitude to Ken Chung, Ketrick Chin
and Veronica Lee (Pulau Sipadan Resort, www.dive-malaysia.com),
Max Ammer (Papua Diving, www.papua-diving.com), Jim & Cary Yanny
(Eco Divers Manado, www.eco-divers.com), Steve & Miranda Coverdale
(Kungkungan Bay Resort, www.divekbr.com), Annabel Thomas
(AquaMarine Diving - Bali, www.aquamarinediving.com),
CRESSI-SUB (www.cressi.it), Willy Volk, Roberto Galli & Laria Bettini

Special heartfelt thanks are also due to Doug Perrine, Charles Hood,
Martin Spragg, John Scarlett, Alex Mustard, Indra Swari Wonowidjojo,
Eric Cheng, Doug Sloss, Leon Joubert & Claudia Pellarini-Joubert,
Will Chen, Roger Horrocks, Tony Wu, Ketrick Chin, Alan J.Powderham,
Stephen Wong & Takako Uno, Fiona Ayerst, Alberto Luca Recchi,
Jason Heller and Rinie Luykx for having generously made their
beautiful images available for this project.

Published by
Nautilus Publishing Sdn. Bhd.
Lot 38, 1st Floor, Block C, Bandar Tyng, Mile 5,
North Road, PPM 255 Elopura,
90000 Sandakan, Sabah, Malaysia
tel: 6089-673999 / 674999
fax: 6089 - 673777

e-mail:
nautilus@streamyx.com
nautiluspub@tin.it

http://www.reefwonders.net

Graphic design: Daniele Clarotto

First printing 2007

ISBN 978-983-2731-02-3

CONTENTS

WHY IN THE WORLD ARE WE DOING THIS?
Some ruminations on underwater photography

I regularly find the dismissive attitude the topside world adopts regarding underwater photographers and their work exceptionally frustrating. No matter how difficult, costly or even downright risky taking photographs in the ocean may be or how objectively splendid the pictures, they will always be given a cursory – if lucky, grudgingly admiring – glance before turning to more "serious" material, like politicians, racing cars and cathedrals. Even the outright admiration occasionally (and usually noisily) expressed by common observers has more to do with the intrinsic alien nature of the subjects and the real or imagined dangers of stalking and framing them, than with the inherent value of the image itself. This is so strange – for a planet 70% covered by sea and which should, in all honesty, be better known as "Water" rather than "Earth", humans seem to care very little, if at all, about the wondrous beauty of the ocean and its mysteries. The sad, inescapable fact is that nowadays the vast majority basically think of the ocean as a wet, windy, dark and dangerous place where fish are simply found only to be caught and eaten in endless quantities and will sustain this attitude until the last stocks are gone (which apparently, from what we hear, will be quite soon). Diving in the sea is strange enough – but taking photographs down there, oh dear, that's only for obsessed amateurs! Oh yes, in our circles we have our own idols – the late Jacques-Yves Cousteau, David Doubilet, Howard Hall, Doug Perrine and a few others. However, all things considered, theirs is a cult mostly practised by other divers, by a close and tightly-knit clique of passionate amateurs and a few inspired professionals united by their very own private love for the sea and its inhabitants. They have been immensely influential of course – thanks to their publications, documentaries, and photographs – but they are exceptions to the rule. Let's face it – it's immensely easier selling a cute picture of a kitten, of a blooming rose, or of a kid playing with a balloon than one of a rare, fascinating, seldom-seen marine creature or a spectacular underwater panorama. Snow-capped mountain ranges, cocktail-toting smiling waiters by bright swimming pools and sunny flowerbeds are welcomed, coral reefs are viewed quizzically and, more often than not, quietly ignored or filed away, even in the editorial offices of most sophisticated travel magazines. It's difficult to accept this when you think that the human race knows almost nothing of the sea and its inhabitants, that the oceans are the last frontier to be explored and that most of the world's new species being discovered today come from the marine environment. And yet, if you don't believe me – just try! Even successful underwater photographers – those who finally satisfy that dark hidden desire secretly haunting every underwater shutterbug in the deepest corner of their heart...publishing! – will usually see their most beautiful images only printed in dive magazines, dive calendars, dive coffee-table books and so on. Essentially, at the end of the day, just within the circles of the diving industry, not in the wider mainstream media. The only logical – and disappointing – conclusion we can reach is that the endless beauty and staggering colour palette of the underwater world – not to mention its scientific load of yet-to-be-tapped knowledge – really seems to fail in eliciting any real interest outside diving circles. It is as if the true nature of the liquid world were a secret only revealed to those willing to explore it, a precious knowledge of beauty destined to remain an incomprehensible, unappetizing mystery to those staying physically away from it. You'll need the gaping, toothy mouth of a Great White Shark to be on a major newsmagazine's cover, and that will happen only once in a lifetime – but how many other incredibly easier, much less interesting and more mundane subjects are published every minute? So, let's face it – underwater photographers are basically destined to be considered a slightly demented branch of a more general breed of weirdoes – i.e. common scuba divers – who obsessively delight in doing extremely uncomfortable things to bring home colourful – and ultimately quite uninteresting – photos of queer-looking places and things. Landlubbers look down on us with the patronizing complacency commonly reserved for surprisingly bright kids – who will be kids nonetheless – and things are not going to change soon.

Ok, that was the depressing part. Now let's get to the real core of the matter – why should we want to take pictures underwater? Well, there are several good reasons. One, the simplest, is to take home pleasant memories of our trips. For these you won't need expensive, sophisticated equipment, nor will you need to drive yourself to extremes, painfully striving to reach the stratospheric standards of the masters. Be your own master and critic – whatever you're happy with is fine, since you're doing it for your own enjoyment, and whatever you take will be good enough for most other people. Get wet, click around and be happy – it's your life after all!

After a while, however, the chances are that you'll start feeling the temptation to emulate the achievements of those wonderful photos you've been seeing in dive magazines and the occasional coffee-table book on marine life. If you want to go a step further then you'll need more complex and costly equipment – and more discipline. You'll have to learn from others and teach yourself a few painful lessons in the process, be willing to accept failure and be obstinate enough to keep trying. You'll also have to spend more money – both in equipment and travelling – but in time, if you try hard enough, you'll start getting great shots. Some of them might even qualify as Art – even if only to your diving peers and not to the land-locked critics. At this stage you will feel the urge to start experimenting, to stretch in new directions, and to try new techniques. It is then that you will have to take your most difficult decisions, choosing between the past simple joys of amateurishness and the demanding intensity of the creative process. Beware, there is a strong lurking danger of missing the fun of it all, once you commit – so take your time and have a good long talk with your inner self before proceeding further.

After that, and only if the results you've achieved have been consistently judged good enough – again, at least by the diving community – you might finally desire to step towards the profession-

als. That step will bring even more hardships and disappointments, tempered by the occasional triumph. But that objective is still a long way off – at least for most of us - so let's stick to the basics for the time being. This means realizing that we divers are all explorers, that every dive – regardless of our level of experience – is another step in a new direction and that we all have the chance of seeing and maybe photographing something mysterious and possibly even unknown. Despite the funny stares we may get on dry land, we are in fact spearheading the exploration of a new world, so incredibly complex, so little documented and yet now so dangerously threatened by uncontrolled human activity. We dive in awe, every time, everywhere and at any depth, and we – as explorers, as pioneers, and, yes, indeed as photographers - have the moral duty to bring back tangible, visible records of what we have experienced, to be shared with the rest of the world, that landlocked world to whom our seas are as forbidding and remote as the reaches of outer space – to share that knowledge, however amateurish and incomplete it may be. Knowledge brings respect, and respect, in turn, gives rise to understanding and ultimately love. And love is what the oceans need today from all of us – for without love there can be no preservation. So how's that for a motivation, eh?

Chapter 1

THE SWORD AND THE HAND
Choose the right tools and learn to use them well

- The Sword of Power
- The Great Nikon vs Canon debate
- Choice of camera and housing
- Film or Digital
- Strobes
- Gadgets
- General scuba equipment
- Maintenance myths - Do's and Don'ts

We have all heard of Excalibur, and some of us will remember Durendal. Many of us will also remember a hirsute barbarian of yore hammering away at the anvil, unfolding the Secret of Steel, forging the red-hot sword which will make Conan, his young son, the Ruler of Cimmeria. Others will think of Andùril, reborn from the broken shards of Narsil, in the Elven halls of Rivendell, and others again will cherish that razor-sharp blade of beauty, the glistening katana fashioned by the master sword-maker Hattori Hanzo to suit the Bride's vengeful needs in Quentin Tarantino's saga, *Kill Bill II*. Ah, the Sword of Power! That

No other natural environment on Earth can probably offer as many immediate, seductive photographic opportunities to the wildlife photographer as a healthy, untouched coral reef does. Bright colors, strange shapes, all kinds of motions and light conditions endlessly and continuously vary, while the sheer numbers of the subjects darting and gliding in every direction can actually even be overwhelming to the casual observer. Most divers can obtain good photographic results in such a rich environment - with a little discipline, a bit of creativity and some experience.

Guest
Photographer

Claudia
PELLARINI-JOUBERT
South Africa

Nikon D100
Nikon 12-24mm
Sea & Sea housing
Sea & Sea YS350 dual strobes

As if conducting the rousing crescendo of an underwater orchestra, the chain-mail suited shark feeder of Claudia's impeccable shot brandishes his bait stick like a wizard's wand - evoking the gaping, toothed maw of the huge shark breaking into the scene from the left, a powerful statement of raw power and muscle, reinforced by the twirling, curving mass of his companions behind the diver. Shark feeding «rodeos» images are often quite unappealing, but in this case the almost techno-industrial setting of the shot - an ugly, naked wreck - adds to its visual strength thanks to the clever use of the theatrical, brash, perfectly positioned spotlight in the background. Unnatural, yes - but also exceptionally striking.

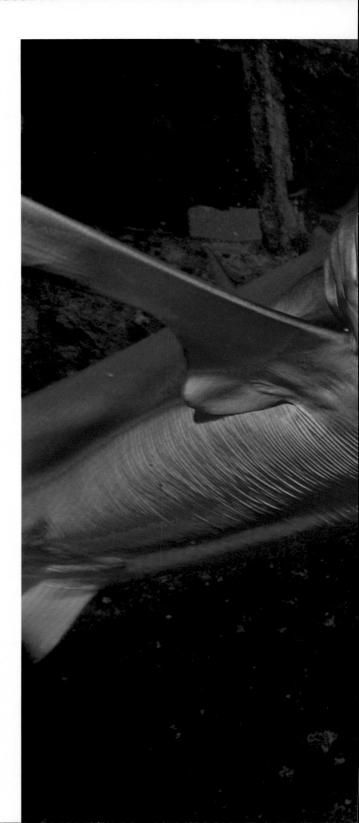

mystical weapon long desired by man, capable of making an invincible warrior out of a frail youth, to conquer foes and subdue kingdoms! Alas – or luckily, depending on how we look at this – such a powerful tool does not exist in real life, as there is no magical paintbrush to make an instant Michelangelo out of us, or an automated keyboard to make us all play like a ready-made Mozart. And yet, too many underwater photographers keep on looking for such an article, and a whole industry is thriving on such a fallacious quest. Hopeless optimism! As the old time knight used to say – it is not the sword which counts, but the hand which wields it! So learn your first lesson – despite whatever you keep on being told, despite all the boasting you might have been hearing, despite all the ballyhoo you've been reading, there's no such thing as the best camera. In fact, there's a huge number of them – so many, and so rapidly and constantly evolving in this wondrous digital era of ours, that it is pretty useless suggesting a particular model here. Do a little informative reading – the technical data, not the blurbs – and pick one. Easy! Even most point-and-shoot little cameras are today superbly equipped for taking wonderful underwater snapshots (as long as there's a housing for them somewhere, so check that first), and if you're good or serious enough to dive with a housed DSLR you certainly do not need my advice here. It's you that's taking the photograph, not the camera. There are a few basics to keep in mind however – you wouldn't want to buy a blunt blade after all, would you? One big – and

▶ text continued on page 21

Large schools of fish invariably - and understandably - leave divers in awe. There are no other places left on Earth - except the ocean - where humans can still interact so closely with such huge numbers of animals in the wild. Choosing the right type of lens for the expected situation of the day is one of the most important aspects of underwater photography - here a 16mm fish-eye lens was used to frame the Tallfin batfish *Platax teira* school to a visionary, almost abstract effect. Good equipment is useless, however, if the underwater photographer is not able to correctly, fluidly interact with his marine subjects.

A (VERY) BASIC PRIMER TO DIGITAL CAMERAS

The digital revolution has taken the world of photography - underwater or not - by storm. In fact, it's not even correct calling it a *revolution* anymore, since it's been firmly entrenched in our daily life for quite some time now. What follows is then not intended to be a guide to digital photography, as that would greatly exceed the scope of this book: it simply is an attempt to clear up a few of the doubts most commonly cast by novices - including those coming from the world of film and doubtfully entering that of digital. For strictly more technical information and regular updating on this frantically evolving technology, several Internet websites and forums are today the best option.

FROM FILM TO DIGITAL

Digital cameras offer quite a few advantages in comparison to analog (film) ones. Two of these, above all the others, concern us as underwater photographers: one, there are no more huge numbers of rolls of easily damaged film to lug around when travelling, and two, the currently available large-size memory cards of DSLRs (Digital Single Lens Reflex) allow taking literally hundreds of images (inside a 4 gigabyte card there's enough room for 670 large size jpegs or 240 raws) in the course of a single dive, in the lucky case you should need them. True, digital camera batteries display voracious appetites, but that can be easily solved by the judicious acquisition and use of rechargeables, and the strobes used in conjunction with them require much less power, lasting consequently longer and recharging faster between one shot and the next. And if the original images are of good quality the much feared dowloading and "workflow" - which always worries first-time digital users - will be smooth, easy and fast, with very little or no tampering at all to be done. The autofocus systems available on current DSLRs and their dedicated lenses are also exceptionally fast, sensitive and reliable when compared to their analog counterparts of the past - a great boon when shooting fast-moving underwater subjects.

QUALITY AND RESOLUTION

But what about quality image and resolution? This matter can be be debated to no end - but the basic truth is that any good-quality point-and-shoot will make most amateur users happy, and several high-quality DSLRs produced by the major brands today are perfectly capable of delivering technically faultless images. Nothing new under the sun here - as in the past, the most advanced (and usually expensive) equipment will offer more flexibility and better technical options.

In the past, one would switch from one kind of film to the next in the quest for the best results both in quality (color tonal range, among others - some loved Kodachrome, others would swear by Fuji) and sharpness (Fuji Velvia 50 was reputed the best choice by most), but now that flexibility is actually part of the camera itself, and is measured - together with a few other factors - by the types of sensor (mainly responsible for image quality) and the number of megapixels (responsible for image size and sharpness) offered by the model. Image quality is rather subjective, but here's a little refresher to what can be expected regarding image size and sharpness when choosing a digital camera:

▶ 2 megapixels and under

Your basic point-and-shoot digital camera. Two megapixels is barely enough to get reasonably sharp A4 and smaller. It's good for holiday snapshots and family portraits you're taking just for yourself - and little else. Toy-like cameras such as these are disappearing fast.

▶ 3 - 3.9 megapixels

These little point-and-shoot will get you reasonably sharp A4 and smaller. Image quality is definitely better and some interesting options are available - at little cost. Still for strictly amateur shots.

▶ 4 - 4.9 megapixels

Advanced point-and-shoot with several extra features. The larger number of pixels allows for minimal cropping of images while still getting a good A4 image.

▶ 5 - 5.9 megapixels

Same as above but with obvious advantages as even wider cropping can be applied. But if you need all that cropping you might also need to seriously review your framing philosophy.

▶ 6 megapixels and above

We're slowly getting there - very large prints, great cropping options, lots of extra features. Above all, an excellent back-up for fast topside shots. You can get truly great images with one of these - but then, you might as well take the extra step, if you're really serious about your underwater photography.

▶ Pro DSLRs

Ranging from 10 to 12 megapixels, this is what you want for professional results - large, razor-sharp images you can print in books, magazines, posters and brochures, or sell through commercial agencies.

DSLR cameras allow you to change lenses, have an incredibly short shutter lag time, exceptionally fast autofocus performance, and great exposure flexibility. Yes, they're bigger, heavier and a lot more expensive - and the full system, including u/w housing, one or two strobes with their arms, and all lens ports, is going to be very costly and quite cumbersome while travelling and diving. But the immense flexibility of the system is what will allow you to take great underwater photography - if you put your mind and soul into it, of course. Today the same number of megapixels is also offered by several pocket cameras - highly sophisticated pieces of machinery and less and less limited in their options. It's worth checking on the availability of u/w housings for some of these if you are interested.

ISO SENSITIVITY

Do not let the exceptionally high range of ISO sensitivity offered by digital cameras trick you, however: it might be very handy for topside shots, but for high-quality noiseless underwater images you should never shoot at settings higher than ISO 100 (the lowest setting offered by most DSLRs, in fact), only switching to ISO 200 for low-level available light situations. Despite all the smart talk, underwater shooting at higher settings will result in noisy images - good for Web use obviously, but not good enough for high-quality professional printing on paper. This is a choice which is entirely up to you, depending on the final destination of your work. "Noise", for those who are not familiar with the term yet, is the digital equivalent of film graininess.

JPEG OR RAW?

In what digital format should you shoot? Again, it depends from the final destination of your images. If you are shooting for yourself, your family and the Internet, jpegs will do. Your memory card will allow you to shoot hundreds of images in one single dive, post-production on your computer will be kept to a bare minimum, storage capacity will not be a problem, and several cameras will even offer a choice between several jpeg quality and size settings. This is the easiest option offered by most point-and-shoots. There's one glitch, however - jpegs progressively degrade in quality with each manipulation (cropping, resizing, color correction, saving and so on), and if you get the shot of a lifetime you won't be able to do much with it, since most commercial photo agencies and publishers won't probably accept it for this reason: every time you do something to the photo, you affect the original image - and there's no way to undo it.

Raws, on the other hand, store a lot more information (requiring more memory), may occasionally look rather unimpressive as shot and need

a little bit more work when being downloaded - but the great advantage with them is that being a "digital negative" they can be stored indefinitely, each time an image is needed the photographer actually saving a more or less modified/enhanced copy in a different format (tiff, jpeg) with no degradation whatsoever to the original raw image itself. Watching the final printed product on a book page today it is quite impossible to ascertain any real difference to the eye between a high-quality original jpeg image and a raw which has been manipulated and later saved as a jpeg or tiff, but the difference lies in the flexibility and longevity offered by the latter. The possibility of shooting in raw will ultimately dictate your choice of camera model once you'll have sorted your priorities as an underwater photographer.

WHITE BALANCE

Being unheard of in the world of film photography, this seems to be one of the main worries of novices - some swear to the "Cloudy" setting (especially with point-and-shoots), others offer complex pre-balancing underwater routines at the start of the dive. Solutions vary, but the easiest is shooting in raw while using a good DSLR - white balance can be then left on the "Auto" setting and any modest adjustment, if needed at all, will be easily and rapidly done in Photoshop when saving the images. This is another of the many life-saving technical comforts offered by the use of raws and high-end DSLRs.

DSLR LENSES

This is tricky - and quite surprising for those used to film - so I'll try to make it as simple as possible. Without getting into the technical details, suffice to say that due to the reduced size of the sensor used by most DSLRs, the nominal focal length of the lenses you were used to is now increased in actual use by a third. The much-loved Nikon AF 105mm becomes a 153mm when used on most DSLRs, and to get a true fish-eye when shooting digital you'll need to abandon your old Nikon AF 16mm, substituting it with the new Nikon D-AF 10.5mm, which compensates for the new parameters of digital and offers the same field of view of the previous lens. Not a big deal really - but be prepared for a transitional period, during which many of your smaller traditional macro subjects, for example, will suddenly loom much too large in your viewfinder. Not many solutions here really - one could back off and shoot from further away (a no-no usually, except in very good visibility, when one could actually turn to tele-macro) or switch to the ubiquitous AF 60mm, which will now frame as a 90mm. Of course one might also turn to micro - rather than macro - photography, discovering new subjects in the realm of the ultra-small! Several new top-of-the-line DSLR models - both Canon and Nikon - are now however offering full-size sensors, eliminating the problem. ∎

U/W PHOTOGRAPHY WITH A POINT-AND-SHOOT CAMERA IN SEVEN EASY STEPS

By Leon Joubert & Claudia Pellarini-Joubert*

If you are reading this, you obviously have a desire to get started in underwater photography - and chances are that, if you're starting from scratch and have no previous experience, a simple point-and-shoot digital camera will be your first tool of choice. But what can you expect from it?

Cameras cost money, and the big DSLRs cost a lot of money. Underwater housings cost even more! When you have to purchase both camera and a housing, you ask yourself: how much am I going to use this in a year? Is it worth forking out big bucks for something that might be obsolete in two years from now anyway? What if I flood this? And so, most people quite justifiably opt for the escape route; an affordable compact "point-and-shoot" housing system that doesn't break the bank.

Herein lies the challenge; obviously the point-and-shoot does not have the capabilities of the DSLR, and so you have to make the most of the features at your disposal. At the end of the day, it is the photographer who creates the image, not the camera. Put a top of the line DSLR system in the wrong hands, and the results can be awful. Working cleverly with a "point-and-shoot" camera, however, it is entirely possible to take breathtaking pictures, making it so much more interesting when people find out you used a cheaper system. There is hope after all; all you have to do is know your camera and adhere to few simple rules…

* Leon and Claudia (www.bittenbysharks.com) have run the video and photo center of Stuart Cove's in Nassau for several years, working with many film and documentary crews, setting up countless shark dives and above all teaching basic underwater photography skills to thousands of novices. They currently reside and work in South Africa.

▶ **Rule 1: Buy the right camera.**

Today there are hundreds of models on the market. The housing manufacturers take a careful look at a few of the most appropriate and popular ones and produce housings accordingly. If you buy the camera you like and wish to go underwater with it in the near future, check first if that particular model "made it" to housing status.
Buy the housing which suits your particular needs and abilities. It is not necessary to buy the most expensive housing; it is more important to be able to add the important accessories as your abilities and needs improve.

▶ **Rule 2: Use an external strobe.**

Most of today's compact cameras are not designed with divers in mind, so the built-in flash is really just a fill light that has virtually no impact under water. It sits too close to the lens anyway which causes backscatter, as it lights up all the floating particles right in front of the lens. The vast majority of divers end up with monochromatic blue-green pictures or even worse; white snow with scary looking blue creatures in the background. The internal flash can work well for macro, but results are not consistent, being so dependant on the length of the particular housing's protruding lens port, and more often than not, the resulting peculiar shadow spoils the image.
If you attach an external strobe, all these problems can be addressed. Strobes vary in size and most strobes will fit most camera housings on the market today. You have the flexibility to use either one or double strobes. Don't worry if your camera does not have a plug point for strobes, most of the smaller ones work via a sensor - whether wired or wireless - that picks up the little built-in flash and fires as you depress the shutter, giving you glorious colour and depth.
A red filter can restore colours lost underwater instead of using a strobe, but the filter has limitations and can only be used in full sunshine and between 3 and 15 meters. Although the camera system is certainly less bulky, the advantages of a strobe outweigh those of the filter. Since it is an "either/or" scenario, choose whichever suits your situation best.

▶ **Rule 3 : Get close to your subject.**

Water absorbs light. Even the most powerful strobe on the market has no impact if you move further than a meter or two away. Smaller strobes made for the smaller camera systems are obviously less powerful, and require you to get even closer than you thought was close in order to be effective. Try to get as close as possible to your subject without chasing it away. If it moves away before you can take the shot, look for something else that doesn't. Use a wide angle converter, if your housing accepts one, in order to achieve well lit wide angle shots.
The lens angle allows you keep everything in frame, while remaining well within your strobe's distance: your point-and-shoot camera is fitted with a lens that is perfect for topside portrait and telephoto shots.
Forget about the zoom button underwater, since your strobe cannot zoom in with you, so what's the point? Zooming in, one only succeeds in degrading image quality anyway. Instead, simply engage the built in "macro button" (the icon of the little flower) for focus at minimum distance. These camera systems are seemingly built for macro. The advantage is that you can get in range of subjects that are usually out of range for DSLRs; like something hidden under a ledge, for example.

▶ **Rule 4 : Try and shoot static or slow moving subjects.**

Everyone wants to shoot a magnificent picture of a free swimming whale shark or a passing pod of dolphins. But by now you should know the limitations of your system and you should shoot accordingly. The light meter of the most basic point-and-shoot camera tends to register slow shutter speeds as a direct result of the distinct lack of light underwater. The result is blur when trying to capture fast moving subjects. Of course the logical answer would be to select a faster shutter speed, in order to freeze the action, but when the camera does not offer a manual option, then you must find a way! And there is a way, at a price of course. Simply increasing the ISO forces the basic camera to use a faster shutter speed, although image quality deteriorates slightly. Reduce noise on a compact camera by keeping the ISO as low as possible, which means (unless you have full manual functions): stick to the static, easy subjects!

▶ Rule 5: Control the camera, don't let it control you.

Most point-and-shoot cameras will offer a variety of shooting modes. Most users will opt for the apparently easy Auto mode, although the best underwater images are achieved when you do not allow the camera to control the exposure. Controlling the exposure can mean learning to use a manual or semi-manual mode; controlling aperture, shutter speed or both - or it can be using the only means your basic camera has on offer. Some cameras have no manual controls, and so the only way to control exposure, is via the exposure compensation button. Find this handy "plus/minus" button and you will regain all the control you need. Because these cameras are primarily for land use, their light meters tend to "freak out" underwater due to the lack of light; the result is a tendency to overexpose almost everything. By regulating the exposure, you regain balance in your image. Most compacts have White Balance options. Some have a function allowing the photographer to set a "customised" white balance, using a white slate underwater. This can cause a dramatic change in some cameras, causing colours to suddenly look more natural.

▶ Rule 6 : Shoot, adjust and shoot again

Gone are the days of 36 pictures in a roll. With the right size media card you are only limited to the battery life of the camera and strobe. Take the liberty to shoot as many shots as you can of the same critter, all the while making adjustments to exposure compensation, White balance, ISO, strobe intensity and position. Because it is not advisable to judge a shot from the small LCD screen only, some compact cameras even have his-tograms that help with determining exposure. More and more compact housings even offer the luxury of TTL. But the best policy (in "point-and-shoot" cameras photography) is to shoot as much as you can in the moment, and review later on the computer afterwards, where you can simply delete the shots not worth keeping.

▶ Rule 7: Half press to focus

All of the point-and-shoot cameras require a "half-press" in order to auto focus. Focusing is what caused the delay on the little cameras. Clicking the shutter means that the camera still has to lock focus and then shoot. Older technology means that the delay is more prevalent. Newer technology means that the delay is not as noticeable as before. If you learn how to half-press to focus first, lock it in by holding the button just there, the next half-press gets you the shot without delay. This can work well with a clownfish, which darts in and out, up and down for instance. But it is not as easy as it seems. The downside with the point-and-shoot housings is that the actual shutter button or lever does not usually have a positive feel, as one would have on an DSLR housing. On the DSLR, one can actually feel the momentum of the actual "squeeze" for precise shooting. With a compact, the best way is to get to know that particular housing's "feel" and become one with your instrument.

At the end of the day, your diving ability will impact your results. And so, whether you opt for a "point-and-shoot" pocket camera or a DSLR, you must be able to control yourself underwater so that you can get where you want to take the shot. It is not the camera system, as much as you! Remember, the ocean is huge, and you may get an opportunity with a compact, that someone with a DSLR does not. Now go out there, take your little pocket camera and hold your head up high. Don't feel intimidated by the big guns - yours will fire just as well! ∎

Martin SPRAGG

Belize

Olympus c5050z
Ikelite housing
Ikelite DS51 strobe

Quick reflexes and a gift for composition are at the origins of this spectacular shot by Martin Spragg, who framed to perfection a dolphin chasing a school of jacks in Belize's clear waters. The ultimate proof that wonderful images can be also taken using a point-and-shoot pocket camera - provided a good set of eyes and a working brain are behind it. The small size of the original image does not allow enlargement, however.

Guest
Photographer

Alan J.
POWDERHAM

United Kingdom

Nikon F4
Nikon 105mm
Nexus housing
Nikon SB105 dual strobes

Cleverly painting a little portrait of a Hairy squat lobster *Lauriea siagiani*, Alan J. Powderham imbues the tiny purple crustacean with the gift of a feisty personality, all bristling hairs and candy-striped glaring eyes - woe to trespassers to my pink sponge kindom! Great care was obviously taken in focusing on the subject's minute eyes - at such small distances depth of field is truly minimal, even at the highest aperture, and a small mistake in judgement can spoil the whole photo.

occasionally quite heated – item of discussion often debated around after-dive tables is the brand of the equipment to select. Since most of this stuff is going to be rather expensive and you'll want to use it for a long time, you might want to pause for a second and think it over before you make your choice. Which – bluntly put – is, Canon or Nikon? Several other big time companies produce wonderful pieces of camera equipment of course, but as soon as you'll start diving in the company of others you'll realize the small universe of underwater photographers is quite evenly split among Canon and Nikon users. Each system has its followers, always ready to swear by its unequalled qualities, but the bottom line is that both are perfectly capable of obtaining excellent

A beautiful but rare subject - rising from the abyssal depths at night, an Emperor nautilus *Nautilus pompilio* is briefly photographed along the shores of Borneo before being released again. Uncommon or highly localized species such as this one often require special (and expensive) trips - usually restricted to professional photographers on assignment.

results in the hands of an amateur and spectacular ones in those of a professional. Nikon lenses are supposed to be marginally better but in all honesty I'd be surprised if anybody could detect a difference looking at the final photo. The level of industrial and technical sophistication reached today by both (and several other) companies makes this discussion a moot point, as both offer a vast array of models to suit all pockets and levels of experience. One word of advice, however – do not blindly go for the latest and most complex (and presumably most expensive) model: bide your time and let somebody else swallow the bait, and then see the results and base your choice accordingly. Several highly-touted and very expensive camera models have been launched with a great deal of ballyhoo by the marketing magicians only to go out of production after a few years (don't forget the disappointing Nikonos RS) or to be superseded in the hands of clever users by smaller, less expensive but equally sophisticated models which followed a short time later. For example, the Nikon D2X may have been an incredible tool when it came out, but the Nikon D200 which immediately followed costs a lot less, weighs a lot less, is much smaller and basically offers the same functions – which in great part are much more than any normal photographer would ever need. In case you're wondering, we've been using Nikon equipment for the past twenty years – after having started with Pentax a long time before that. Keep in mind that once you've chosen a system you'll have to stick to it – lenses, hous-

Splendidly camouflaged on the bottom of the Strait of Lembeh in Northern Sulawesi, Indonesia, a grotesque Weedy scorpionfish *Rhinopias frondosa* stares cantankerously at the camera - strangely beautiful in its laced livery and coming in many striking colors, this species is a Holy Grail for underwater photographers worldwide. Professionals and passionate amateurs in search of strange, rare subjects can actually help in environmental conservation, creating job opportunities in local communities and generating economic interest in otherwise neglected marine areas.

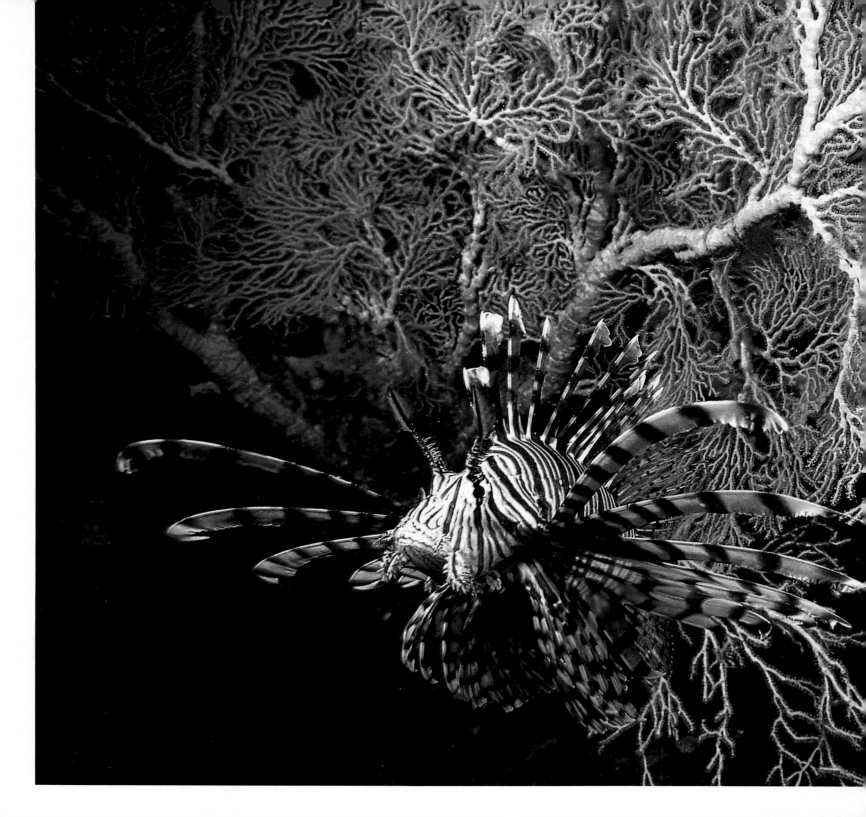

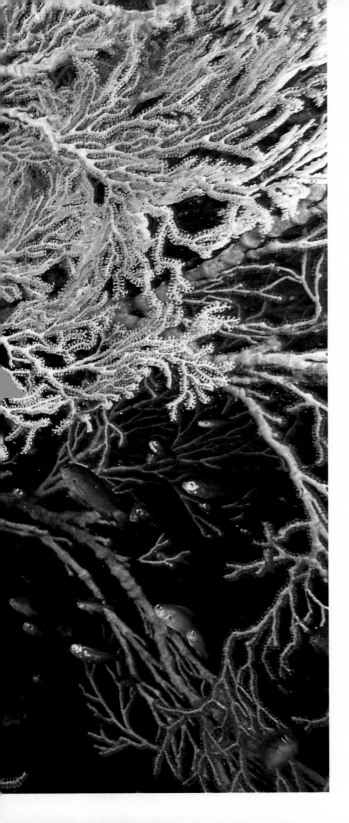

ings and on a lesser scale strobes are hardly interchangeable between systems, and if correctly kept and maintained your equipment will last you a lifetime. Having said that, you have to realize that your choice of camera and brand might also be influenced by the availability of a housing to take it underwater – several models are available today, many being offered by mainstream companies like Sea & Sea, Ikelite or Aquatica and others by smaller scale ones like Subal, Seacam, HugyFot or Nexus. All of these companies can however offer products of the highest manufacturing quality. Again, there's a ridiculous tendency among underwater photographers to strenuously defend the respective merits of their own housings – sporting a snazzy hand-made and incredibly expensive European housing equals to showing up in a Ferrari on Saturday night, and you will soon notice that those belonging to the exclusive circle of big-time professionals tend to all stick to the same "fashionable" label of the day. Both solutions have their ups and downs: commercial housings produced by Sea & Sea or Ikelite offer ease of maintenance, international distribution, constant availability of spares, extensive and occasionally very useful accessories; "roadsters" designed and produced by smaller firms generally look much more beautiful, can be occasionally customized (at a price – and do you really need that?) and are usually a bit more refined in the finishing. Bottom line is, a housing has to keep the camera in and the water out, and as long as it does that it's ok – all commercial housings available

Gracefully hovering by the large gorgonian in the background, a large Common lionfish *Pterois volitans* slowly glides in curiosity towards the camera lens, its wide, banner-like, venomous dorsal and pectoral fins spread out in a threatening display. Underwater photographers should always try to learn as much as possible about their subjects before attempting to approach them closely - as they will almost always have to do in the effort to increase image sharpness. Several common marine species are quite capable of inflicting serious damage to human intruders if provoked or harassed - usually by biting or by inflicting envenomation.

Guest
Photographer

Indra
SWARI WONOWIDJOJO

Indonesia

Canon 350D
Canon 100mm
Sea & Sea housing
Sea & Sea YS120 dual strobes

Many - including the two of us - have taken reasonably good shots of mating Mandarinfish *Neosynchiropus splendidus*, but very few underwater photographers have succeeded where Indra has triumphed - freezing in pitch-black midwater, as if in bottomless, deep outer space, the frenzied fighting of two male Mandarinfish vying for the favours of a female. Blazing erect fins - which at the end of the tournament will have been sadly shredded to pieces - and fluorescent, psychedelic liveries spectacularly enhance the clashing fish, rearing like miniature medieval knights less than five centimeters long. A perfectly framed and sharply focused nocturnal tapestry - achieved with great patience and untiring determination.

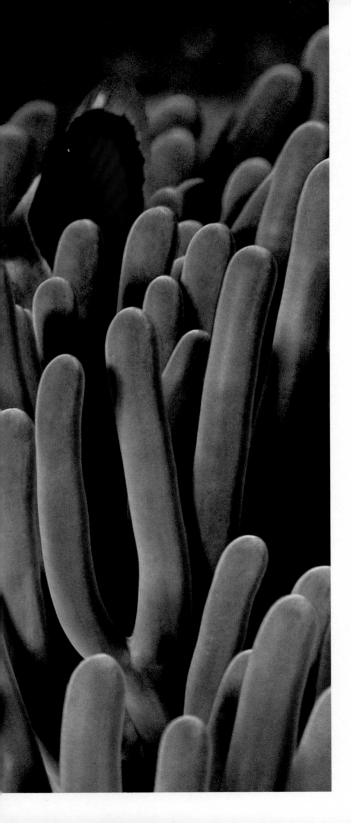

today have reached a high level of accuracy in manufacture and will keep disaster at bay if properly used. Some are bulkier and heavier than others (remember, a small one will be negatively buoyant underwater as it traps less air inside!), some offer add-on enlarging viewfinders for an easier viewing and framing of the subject while others sport pretty small eyepieces - but these are details for each customer to personally assess and live with in the field (add-on viewfinders, for example, are very useful but can be incredibly expensive). I have been diving for fifteen years with my old Nikon F4 in a literally hand-made beautiful HugyFot housing. This had great ease of use and wonderful results (so that might make you lean towards the smaller scale designers – with its shiny oven-baked automotive car lacquer finish I was the envy of fellow divers everywhere!). However, I've recently chosen a mass-produced Sea & Sea housing for my D200 as it offers several advantages compared to other digital housings – very compact size, tough metal body, the possibility of shooting in digital TTL and a very competitive price. As for switching from film to digital, this is again a moot point as you cannot stop innovation. Film (we exclusively used Fuji Velvia 50) has served us exceptionally well in the past, but the gnawing worry of not being able to see the results till we were back from a trip and the anguishing hassle of carrying dozens of film rolls through X-ray machines in these times of difficult, restricted flying had simply become too much. Since we like to think of ourselves as advanced amateurs,

Known by many, loved by all, photographed by most - the Western clown anemonefish *Amphiprion ocellaris* can be closely approached when snuggling among its anemone host's venomous, stinging tentacles. Notice how the high aperture setting at f.22 has resulted in a black background. A macro lens - usually a 60mm or a 105mm - on a housed DSLR is the best choice for shooting small subjects underwater, as most point-and-shoots do not allow a close enough approach. Learning about marine species behavior is a highly enjoyable and interesting aspect of underwater photography, as direct field observation is immediately accessible to those willing to learn.

Guest
Photographer

Martin
SPRAGG

Belize

Olympus c5050z
Ikelite housing
Ikelite DS51 strobe

A wonderfully atmospheric portrait of a balloon jellyfish, floating against the cosmic galaxy / surface sunburst as some alien organism from outer space - a great reminder of what great images can be achieved by little point-and-shoot cameras. Many nitpickers would worry or complain about the slightly burnt highlights at the center of the sunburst, but those certainly do not detract from the general quality of the image - which was taken for personal enjoyment and not for commercial use.

Will
CHEN
USA

Canon 5D
Canon 16-35mm zoom
Ikelite housing
Ikelite DS125 dual strobes

An impossibly graceful underwater ballet in monochrome - two Mantas *Manta birostris* mirroring each other like ghostly, floating draperies drifting in the darkness of Kona's night. Sharp framing and a very soft, unobtrusive lighting contribute to the strange dream-like quality of this highly unusual image - wide-angle shots taken at night are quite uncommon and technically difficult to achieve.

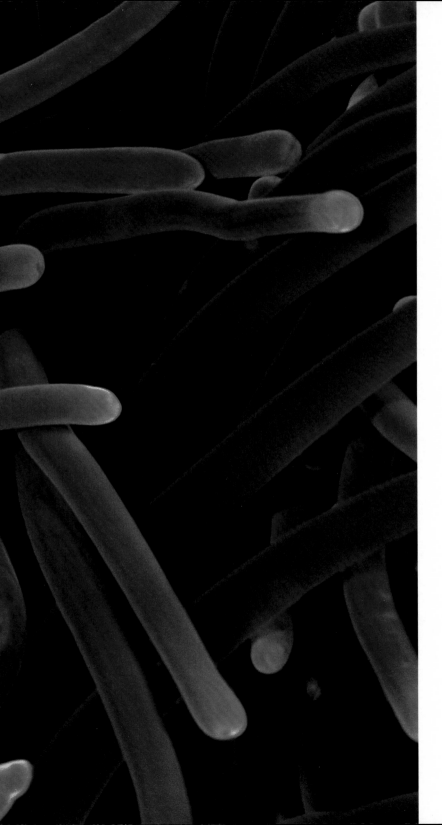

we shoot in Raw and expect to slightly adjust our photos in post-production later, provided of course the shots are worth keeping. The amount of work we do in Photoshop basically amounts to what the technicians at the lab did developing our rolls, so there's no big change there – but more of this later. One very important aspect you might want to consider when choosing a housing for your camera is the capability of the housing itself to accept two strobes (even if you can sometimes use an adapter to use two strobes when your housing offers only one connecting plug) and the positioning of your strobe arms – make sure it's compatible with well-designed arms with comfortable, strong clamps (after a lifetime of frustrations we've happily settled for the very expensive but highly reliable ones produced by Technical Lighting Systems). Strobes have also been greatly affected by the digital revolution – no more need for huge, heavy, bulky and monstrously powerful flashes! Small, lightweight units like those designed today by Sea & Sea or Inon are much preferable to the bigger and more sophisticated models hand-crafted by smaller companies, as ease of maintenance, access to spare parts, simplicity of construction and saving in weight and space are of paramount impor-

A Western clown anemonefish *Amphiprion ocellaris* peeks out of the velvety mass of its softly-hued - yet deadly - anemone host. Much loved by all, clownfish are common but not particularly easy photographic subjects - being extremely mobile within the restricted range of their territory. It takes a lot of practice and a degree of concentration to photograph them as one truly desires, as here, even if their anemone hosts can offer endless interesting chromatic variations. This image was chosen as the cover shot of our book *Oceani Segreti*, which was awarded the World Grand Prize at the Festival of the Underwater Image in Antibes, France, in 2004.

tance for travelling photographers. We used to work with the always-reliable and very powerful Sea & Sea 350s, but nowadays prefer the smaller Sea & Sea 120s, which additionally offer the advantage of AA rechargeable batteries. When building a camera system it is also very important – at least in our experience – to minimize compatibility problems, so it's attractive to stay with a brand which offers as many items as possible, especially now that digital protocols often differ greatly from each other. Try thinking a lot in advance and plan carefully, but when you're happy with one brand, stick to it! We try to keep things as light as possible whenever we travel (we never check in any of our photographic equipment – it's only carry-on LowePro backpacks for us), so we also take our iMac and LaCie hard disk along, and nothing else. Since we feel strongly against useless gadgets – even if we keep on meeting fellow divers draped in those aplenty – I'll add that I'd dive naked if I could, as being one with the surrounding environment is one of the most obvious "secrets" of successful underwater photography. Drifting unencumbered by hanging trinkets and being able to move smoothly and quietly without being snagged on corals by cords, lanyards and such is a primary objective – so no BCDs overloaded with useless D-rings, loose octopus regulators flying

Nudibranchs - also known as sea slugs - are common, easy and incredibly colorful creatures - the ideal subject for beginning macro photographers. As with many other easily photographed marine animals, it is almost impossible resisting the temptation to slowly build up a collection of them - their abstract, dazzling patterns and colors, often evolved to advertise their toxicity to predators, have few rivals in the underwater realm. Several new species have been described and identified thanks to the tireless efforts - and sharp eyesight - of underwater photographers, always keen to "bag" new subjects.

Guest
Photographer

Fiona
AYERST
South Africa

Nikon F100
Nikon 16mm fish-eye
Sea & Sea housing
Sea & Sea YS 120 dual strobes

Emerging from the gloom of Aliwal Shoal's submerged peaks in South Africa, a Sand tiger *Odontaspis taurus* - locally know as «Raggie» or Ragged-tooth shark - bares a Cheshire cat-like toothy smile, its curved fangs gleaming in the darkness which surrounds it. A faultless portrait of a mellow but vastly impressive shark, atmospherically framed against the castle-like ramparts in the background: minimal strobe lighting from below and just a faint hint of the sun, far away in the distance above, add to the distinctly gothic feeling of the image, which well captures the peculiar vampire-like features of the big nocturnal predator.

Several commonly encountered underwater subjects - such as the *Scorpaenopsis oxycephala* scorpionfish illustrated here - are eminently collectable, offering countless variations in color and patterns within the parameters of the species. Building a photographic collection of these can be highly entertaining - one never knows what new unexpected variations are in store! In this particular case, the constant and methodical photographing of scorpionfish has led us to the discovery of a recurring "false mouth" pattern above the eyes of these superbly camouflaged ambush hunters, most probably evolved to confuse potential prey.

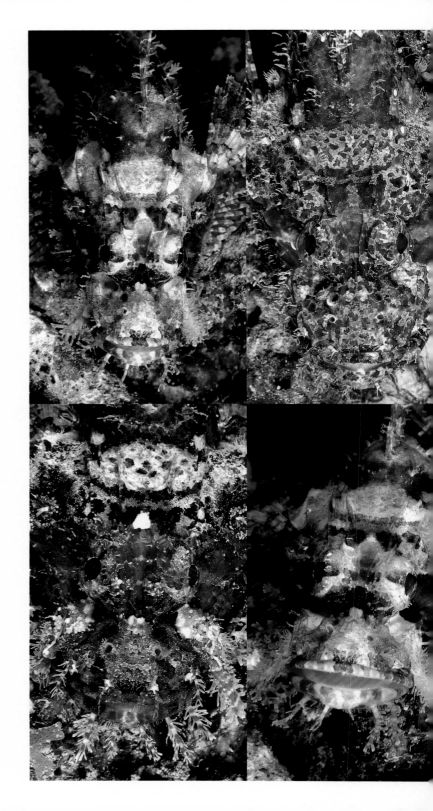

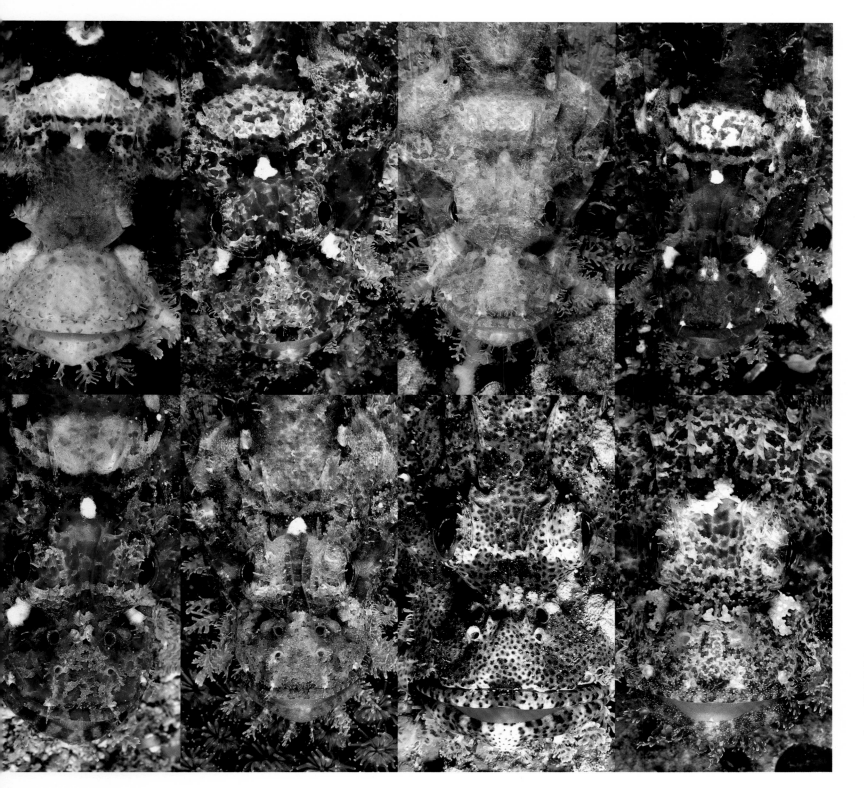

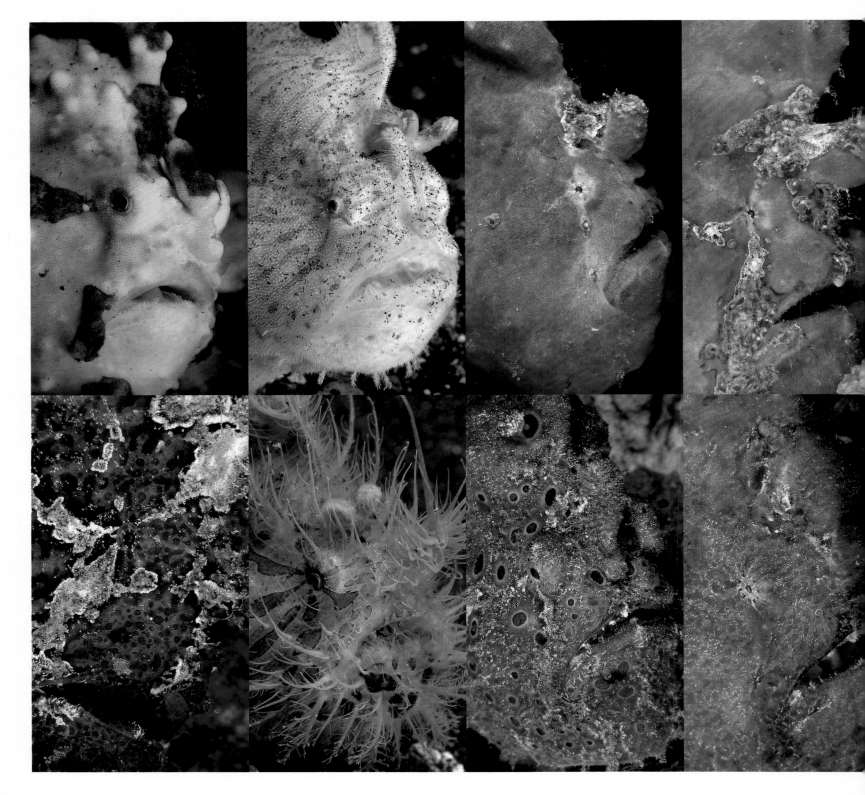

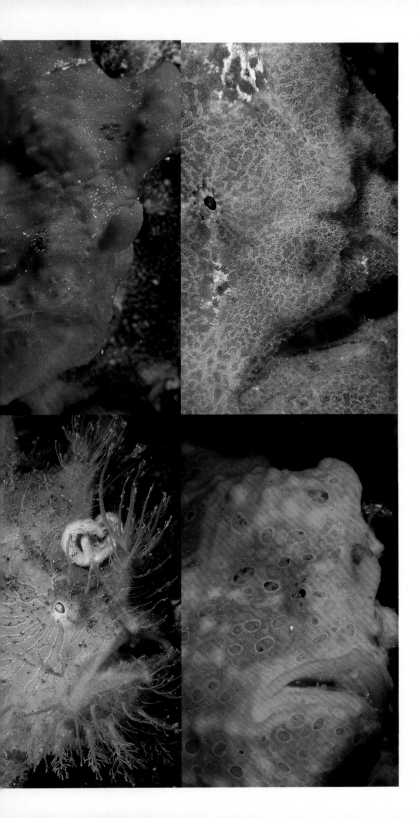

Another eminently collectable photographic subject, frogfish of many different species display an hypnotic variability in pattern and color. Given their extremely peculiar, highly sculptured facial features, frogfish are best portrayed in three-quarters views from the front, occasionally resorting to uneven lighting to obtain dramatic effects and trying to frame them against a deep black background. When building a photographic collection, it is highly advisable to adopt one style of framing and stick to it as much as possible to ensure uniformity.

around and other useless, embarrassing and potentially dangerous gadgets for us. A slim BCD, a small instrument console (preferably tucked in) and a clamp to keep your octopus close to your body will suffice in most situations – always keep extra items (a small emergency torch, an inflatable floating device) tightly packed away in your BCD pockets. This may sound gratuitous and simple-minded advice to the experienced underwater photographer, but you'd be surprised at the number of people we've seen getting stuck, losing stuff, breaking corals and generally making fools of themselves either on a dive boat or underwater. For the same reason I tend not to use a safety lanyard to keep my camera and strobes fastened to myself – should a serious life-threatening emergency present itself I want to be able to ditch every-thing and think of more serious things than saving my camera (but that should be a truly terrifying situation indeed!). Rather more serious – and important – is the much-debated question of maintenance. People, once more, seem to go to ridiculous extremes regarding this matter and for many it is apparently cloaked in a peculiar mystique. We've wit-nessed scores of divers religiously dismantling every single o-ring in their housing in the evening, obsessively greasing each and every one, only to flood everything first thing in the morning. Of course! It worked fine before – why tamper with it? I do not pretend to offer any equipment-saving advice here, and what works for me might be com-pletely unacceptable for others, but in more than twenty years of tak-

A large Scalloped hammerhead *Sphyrna lewini* female curves in for a close look at Cocos Island, Costa Rica - a fleeting, unexpected opportunity which resulted in an overly dark background for an otherwise interesting image. The wrong aperture setting - but, as the saying goes - shoot first, think later! Large sharks - much feared by non-divers - are in fact exceptionally shy and difficult subjects, uncommonly observed and rarely approachable. Their current predicament - being taken to the brink of extinction by the practice of finning and general worldwide overfishing -has been brought to the world's attention by the untiring efforts of the underwater photographers global community.

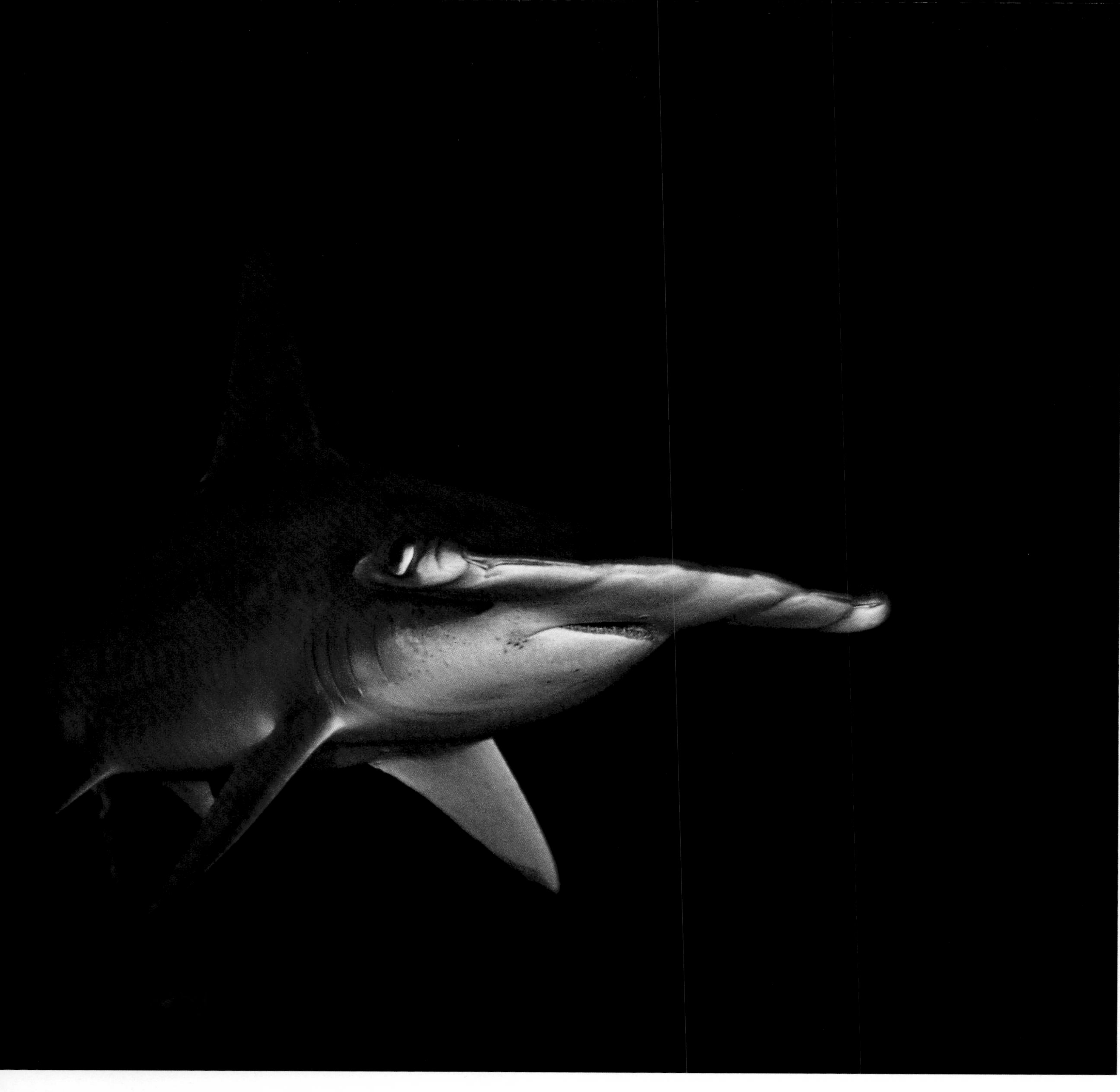

ing photographs underwater I have never flooded a camera or a housing, and the only disaster I've ever had during all these years has occurred when I simultaneously flooded my two strobes at the start of a dive – having blissfully forgotten I had taken the o-rings out for storing after my previous dive trip! So my advice is: one, never take o-rings out of camera housings and strobes before storing away your equipment, even if you're not planning to use it for another six months. Despite what you read on instructions, I never heard of o-rings being deformed by sitting in their groove – provided you store your equipment away at the right temperature after having lightly greased them. The risk of forgetting you took them out is always there! Two, if at all possible never service your equipment before leaving for a dive trip – things move around in bags and some pieces of equipment – such as camera housings – must be forcibly left open to avoid pressurization problems at high altitude. Once you get to your dive destination get a good night's sleep and, the day after, find yourself a good clean table in a well-lit spot. Always put a white, smooth, lint-free towel on the table, set your equipment (silicone grease tubes, o-ring plastic remover tool, paper Kleenex box) like you were preparing surgical instruments for a brain transplant and start working – be methodical, work alone and in religious silence. Get into the "warrior monk" mood – you're sharpening and oiling your sword so that it will not betray you at the moment of truth. You want to do this once, but it's a very important procedure

The right lens, the right place and the right time - in this case a housed 105mm at Puri Jati in Bali: we have been the first ever to document the mating behavior of the Mimic octopus *Thaumoctopus mimicus* in the wild. The whole thing took place in less than 30 minutes at a depth of three meters, requesting the expenditure of a full 36-poses roll of film. A digital camera would have obviously provided more, without forcing us to worry about remaining available shots. Good underwater photographers learn from experience to immediately recognize lucky, unexpected opportunities - and to keep cool when they occur. In this case the difficulty was using a close-up lens as the 105mm from a distance to be able to fully frame the Mimics - opening it at f.5.6 and trying to keep everything in focus.

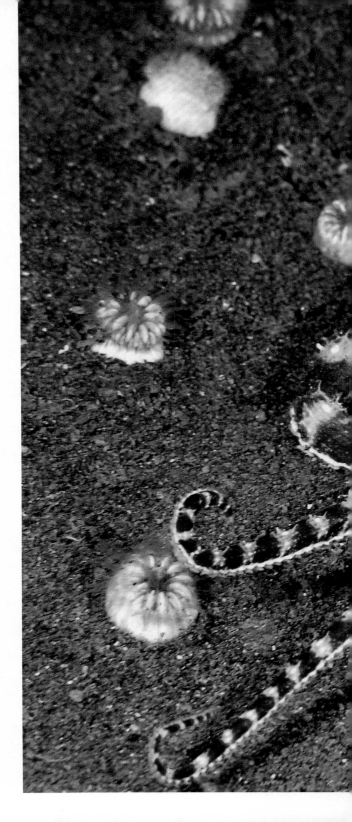

Eric
CHENG
USA

Canon IDs
Canon 180mm
Seacam housing
Ikelite DS125 dual strobes

An adult Clark's anemonefish *Amphiprion clarkii* energetically aerates its egg clutch in a beautifully captured behavioral shot by Eric Cheng - the tiny eyes of the fry, almost ready to hatch, clearly discernible in a carefully captured and accurately composed extreme close-up. Successfully blending scientific accuracy, emotional content and a teeny-weeny bit of that agreeable and unavoidable «cuteness» inherent to clownfish, this is the ideal science-project photo, an ambassador of the wonders of marine life to land-locked viewers.

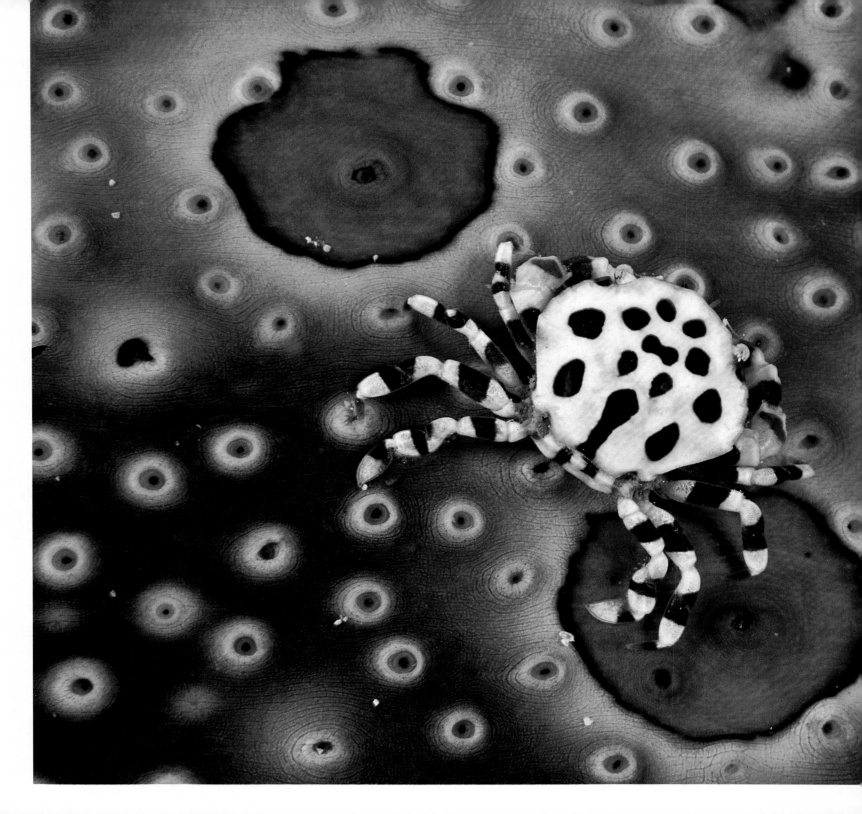

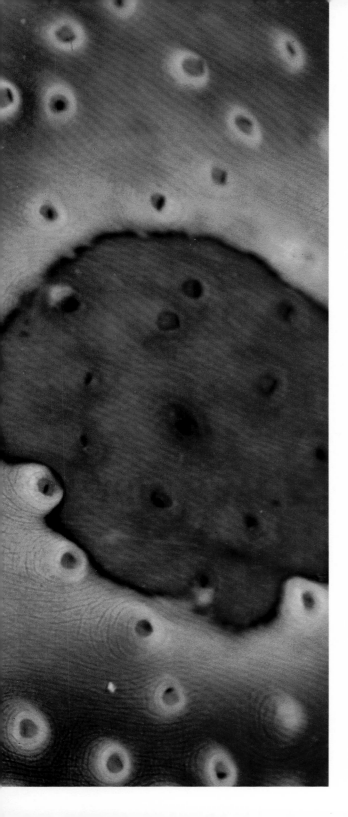

and you do not want to commit mistakes. Apply a little silicone grease on the o-ring, slide it carefully and repeatedly between your very clean fingertips to spread it evenly and make sure there are no impurities (sand, hair and other terrible stuff) whatsoever on its surface, and then replace it in its seat after having lightly passed the corner tip of a lint-less tissue along the length of the groove to get rid of any past deposits. Check carefully the correct seating of the o-ring, check correct alignment of backs, lids or whatever you're going to clamp shut and then, after having closed everything, finally check if the circuitry and gears are working properly (do the switched-on strobes give you the "ready" signal? Does the "ready" flash sign inside the camera viewfinder light up? Do all external camera controls respond correctly? Does the zoom/manual focus gear mesh smoothly? Does the lens autofocus work correctly?). Once you've done this properly – and you'll soon discover that on your first dive of the day, especially if you forget to do a pre-dive trial dip in the freshwater rinse tank! – there's no need to do it again for another week or ten days as long as you take good care of your equipment. Which means:

One, never letting it sitting somewhere by itself – would a warrior let his own sword lie around somewhere? – especially when other divers are present, since people can be exasperatingly careless, particularly when somebody else's equipment is involved. Never, ever leave your set-up sitting unattended on the floor or on a table's corner – don't ever take your eyes off it!

A commensal crab *Lissocarcinus orbicularis* ambling on the surface of its sea cucumber host. When doing macrophotography the right lens is not enough - one has to develop an instinctive grasp for composition, being able to instantly recognize interesting shapes and patterns. Underwater macrophotography can be a demanding activity, requiring much patience, very good eyesight and a mandatory marine biology background - but the results are often highly interesting. On the other hand, it can be easily practiced in shallow, quiet waters in mediocre visibilty and overcast weather - offering the opportunity to greatly increase one's knowledge of the marine environment.

Two, never let anybody else carry it for you to the dive boat or somewhere else.

Three, never let it bump and be kicked around on the bottom of the boat but always find yourself a sturdy plastic basket instead to keep it in (both to avoid other divers tripping on it and to avoid them stepping on its ever-so-sensitive strobe cables).

Four, be very strict and clear in your instructions to whoever will pass you the camera once you're in the water, as lots of inexperienced boatmen will glibly grab the strobe connecting chords thinking they're lanyards or something (of course you don't want to jump in the water holding your camera – that's one of the best ways to flood it right away).

Five, exercise the utmost caution when you open your housing to download your memory card or change the battery – try to do this in a sand-free environment and always wipe yourself reasonably dry to avoid any drops of saltwater or sweat falling on the camera body or into the housing from your hands or brow: this is a very, very tricky time and it pays to be extra careful!

From one side of the scales to the opposite - a gigantic Whale shark *Rynchodon typus*, the largest fish living in the ocean today, glides like a swiftly moving Zeppelin towards the camera (20mm, f.8) at Pulau Lankayan, in Malaysian Borneo. Chance open-water encounters such as these call for available ambient light photography, wide-angle (not fish-eye) lenses and small, handy cameras - a cumbersome set-up could easily prove counter-productive in this case. On the other hand, depth of field is not a guarantee of sharp focusing with such a rapidly moving creature - a fast, reliable autofocus system is then a must. As usual, at the end of the day it is the photographer who makes the difference - not the camera system.

Guest
Photographer

Alberto Luca
RECCHI

Italy

Nikon F4
Nikon 15mm fish-eye
Nexus housing
Isotta 33 dual strobes

Flashing against the ocean's surface off San Diego in California, the stiff, steely torpedo of an aggressive Mako shark *Isurus oxyrinchus* zooms threateningly above, an instant before chomping down on the photographer's strobe. Brilliantly capturing the shark's salient and most striking features - the sharply pointed nose, the gaping fanged mouth, the strongly keeled tail peduncle - Alberto's image paints a picture of power, speed and urgency in almost monochromatic, metallic, glinting tones. This is instinctive power-shooting at its primeval best - the visually and viscerally overwhelming portrait of a terrifying, unrelenting predator in action.

Six, and possibly most important of all, don't ever let your camera and strobes sit in the rinsing tank together with other people's equipment after a dive. Expensive lens domes get ruinously scratched, sensitive TTL coiled strobe cables get pulled to oblivion and apocalypse-proof secure housing latches get pushed open by hideous kids retrieving their disposable one-shot cameras. This may sound ridiculous again, but you cannot believe how many flooding accidents we've witnessed which took place inside rinsing tanks. Instead, try to get there first, grab your set up by the elbows of the securely tightened strobe arms, and push it energetically in and out a few times to give it a good rinsing, then take it out and carry it to your room to quietly dry out in the shade. Then – and only then – you will be allowed to join the other divers, by now freshly showered, spruced up and having a gargantuan lunch. But no complaining – you wanted to be an underwater photographer, right?

A large black manta *Manta birostris* swoops by while Antonella poses in the background, adding depth and interest to an otherwise rather bland image. When working with a model, the latter's capability to anticipate your thoughts and subsequient course of action is of the utmost importance - it is well worth trying to plan actions and reactions in advance whenever possible, at least in a general sense. We tend to avoid mixing divers and marine animals - being by far much more interested in the latter - but there are cases - especially when portraying large animals - where a discreet human presence in the background may actually improve the shot by adding a sense of proportions.

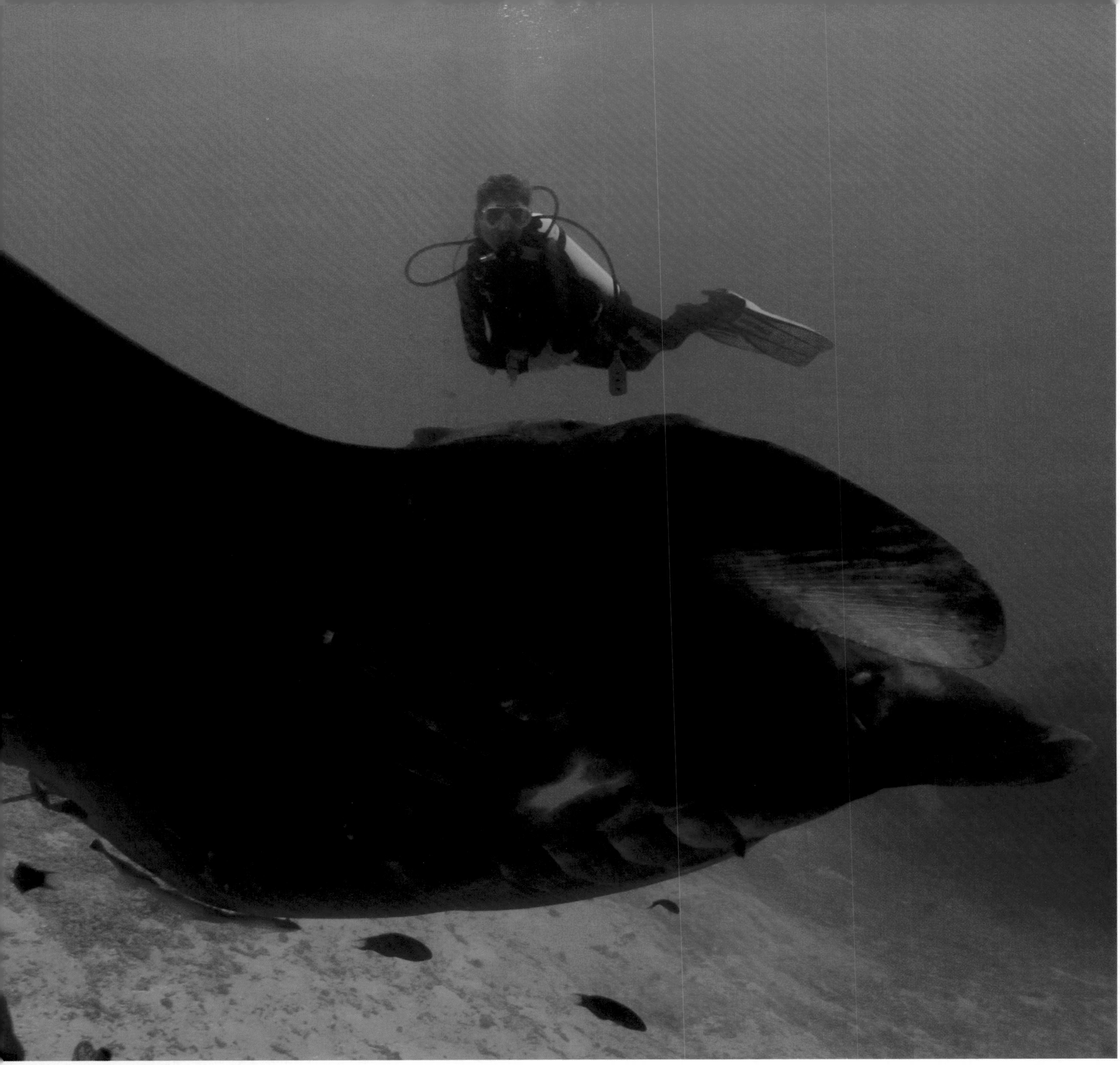

Chapter 2

ZEN AND THE ART OF UNDERWATER PHOTOGRAPHY
Adopting a new frame of mind

- Why do we do this?
- One bullet, one shot
- Rediscovering sportsmanship
- Zen and the art of archery
- The rebirth of instinct through discipline
- Melting away and forgetting oneself underwater

Whatever our motivations in diving with a camera might be, sooner or later we'll have to ask ourselves – as with anything else in life – what our real reasons are. Some of us simply want to bring a nice memory home, some have the desire to create works of art instead, some others feel the urge to document the unknown, and some others have other and presumably equally respectable motives. I certainly cannot imagine what yours are, but after much ruminating and a lot of time spent taking photos underwater I've come to the conclusion that I do this simply because I like it – which isn't as stupid as it sounds. Doing

An Eyespot blenny *Ecsenius ops* peeks warily from the burrow in a mound coral it has inherited from a tube worm. To shoot such a simple but arresting image one needs a good eye for details (to recognize an opportunity when it presents itself - here the striking contrast between the bright yellow eyes of the goby and the surrounding green coral), a great deal of enthusiasm and patience (to scrutinize apparently insignificant subjects - in this case the interesting, sculpted pattern offered by the coral polyps cups) and fast, instictive reflexes (to capture exactly what is but a fleeting instant - the moment at which the tiny fish points both of its independent eyes at the camera).

Guest
Photographer

Roger
HORROCKS
South Africa

Nikon D200
Nikon 12-24mm
Sea & Sea housing
ambient light

There is a lyrical, magical quality to this image of two alien jellyfish silently, slowly swimming among the pillars of a kelp forest near Cape Town: a frigid fairy tale out of outer space, a ghostly - and yet curiously peaceful - reminder of the mystery awaiting all divers in the cloisters of the deep. Notice how the converging lines of the background contrast with the diagonal pattern offered by the two diaphanous main subjects - and how the slanting rays of light blend everything together. It takes well-tuned instincts to recognize such fascinating subjects in the mystical, cool and slightly oppressive stillness of the kelp forest, and a good eye for composition to get away with such an idiosyncratic framing - as shots from above are notoriously difficult to pull off.

Alan J.
POWDERHAM

United Kingdom

Nikon F4
Nikon 60mm
Nexus housing
Nikon SB105 dual strobes

Eyes bulging in terror, its mouth open in a horrified and horrifying silent scream, a shrimp goby lives its last desperate moments as a demon-eyed lizardfish coldly swallows it alive - there is no hope left for the struggling defenceless prey, snatched by the tail in a lightning dash by the sharp-eyed hunter. It is very difficult not to anthromorphize this clinical portrait of life and death momentarily entwining on the reef, a fleeting, revealing glimpse of the dramatic fight for survival sharply caught - in the space of a few precious seconds - by the author's finely attuned instinct.

Guest
Photographer

Alex
MUSTARD
United Kingdom

Nikonos V
Nikonos 15mm fish-eye
ambient light

Like organic flying saucers from outer space, three Southern stingrays *Dasyatis americana* glide in unison towards Alex Mustard's fish-eye lens, their menacing Darth Vader-ish looks amplified by the dark watery horizon they have emerged from. Several elements converge in this image to create a striking portrait - the total absence of any above-water space, the positioning of the three subjects in relation to the photographer and to each other, the bare emptiness of the undulating sand bottom, and the conscious creative decision by the author to opt for black and white. All are finely balanced and captured in a simple yet striking blend in which technique successfully meets instinct.

Guest
Photographer

Tony
WU

Japan

Canon 1D MkII
Canon 15mm fish-eye
Subal housing
ambient light

It takes a great deal of physical stamina to free dive with Humpback whales *Megaptera novaeangliae* in the open ocean of Tonga as Tony Wu loves to do, but the results of his photographic essays can often be absolutely staggering. This shot of a big individual "clapping" is enormous fins (hands?) captures wonderfully the exhilaration of the moment and the fascinating behavior of these intelligent, endangered behemoths of the ocean. To be able to obtain good images of such demanding creatures in such a demanding environment one needs to be greatly focused and strictly disciplined.

things one likes in life is very important, and it also is the best guarantee one will achieve decent results – this will not happen when you're not happy with what you're doing. I like it, and doing it I'm happy – in my case I achieve contentment because I find myself completely immersed in nature, fully removed from the world of the so-called civilized man, being one with the surrounding wilderness, almost erasing my individuality, forgetting my daily earthly worries, my conscious being. Sometimes I even feel like I'd want to fade away, to melt, to disappear into that liquid nothingness – becoming one with the universe. This is a feeling many divers – photographers or not – commonly share, even if not many are actually willing to discuss it. Another and very different source of joy comes however from the remorseless indulging in a basic instinct which I normally find absolutely revolting, i.e. the primeval urge to hunt and kill. Let me be very clear – I totally abhor any sort of hunting and killing animals of any type in the name of a so-called "sport". However, deep inside I'm still an animal myself, as we all are, and I have to come to terms with that. Through the viewfinder of my camera I then succeed in achieving a sublimation of that animalistic, predatory basic desire, in experiencing that adrenaline rush whose deepest roots can be traced to our morally unbiased ancestors of a remote antiquity. So yes – on the surface I'm trying to achieve a satisfying photographic result, and yet at the same time, at a deeper level, I'm freely indulging in a simpler – and yet emotionally and

Good underwater photography does not necessarily always request imposing or colorful creatures - as long as one has eyes and is willing to use them creatively to recognize beauty in emptiness. This Japanese garden-like portrait of tropical serenity has everything coral reefs can offer, except lots of gaudily colored fish: but the transparent stillness of the water and the amazingly articulate reef structures make up for their absence, creating an image of rarefied, mysterious, serene tranquility. Notice how the reflections on the flat, calm surface of the water add to the dimension of quiet of the image.

Guest
Photographer

Rinie
LUYKX

The Netherlands

Canon EOS 5D
Canon 15mm fish-eye
Seacam housing
ambient light

A portrait in stillness pervaded by an almost mystical atmosphere, this frozen fairy-tale wasteland - in fact a thriving oyster bed in the Annajacobapolder in the Oosterschelde - immediately brings to the mind the desolate wintry landscapes painted by Pieter Bruegel, muted featureless panoramas suspended in time, fading away in the distance. Diving in cold, murky waters which are almost devoid of colorful subjects requires dedication and motivation - qualities to which Dutch underwater photographer Rinie Luykx adds a very personal, poetic quality of his own in the treatment of light, no doubt subconsciously inherited by the great painting tradition of his country.

Guest
Photographer

Ketrick
CHIN

Malaysia

Nikon D2X
Nikon105mm
Nexus housing
Inon Z220S dual strobes

Pygmy seahorses *Hippocampus bargibanti* rival clownfish among some of the ocean's most loved and photographed creatures - yet, by longtime finely tuned reflexes, Ketrick Chin has succeeded in portraying one doing the unexpected. Suspended in the black void between the sanctuary of two gorgonian perches, his tiny subject is both a portrait of elegance as it is of frailty, a symbol of the sea's beauty and at the same time of its dangers.

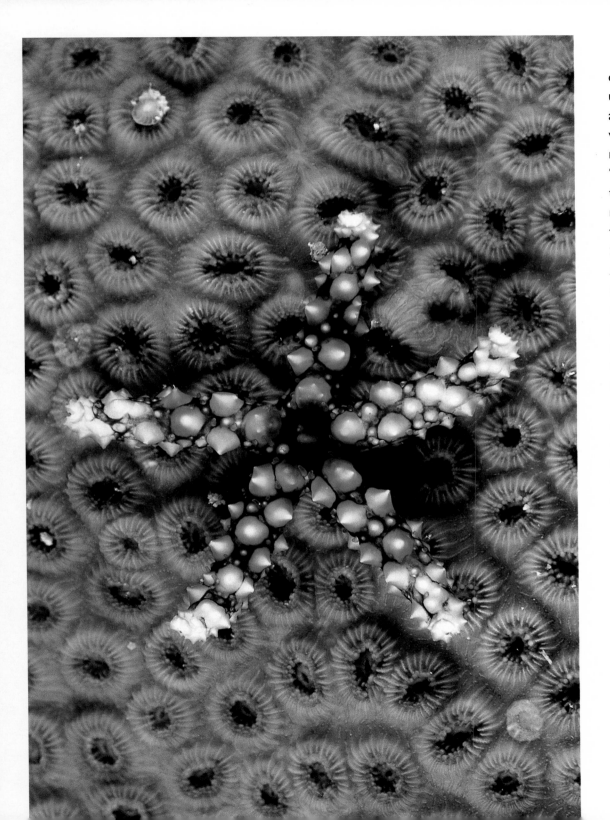

culturally very significant — pleasure: the joy of unabashedly peeling away that skin of self-control which, Jekyll-like, controls and measures our daily behaviour. "*Gotcha! I nailed you!*" I am, essentially, rediscovering and laying bare my animal instincts, just like a new-found Mr. Hyde, staying with the Stevenson characters analogy. Again, I have the gut feeling this attitude is — consciously or not — shared by a great many underwater photographers, who have metaphorically or not hung up their spear gun on the wall and taken up the camera in its place.

At the same time, I'm also experiencing great pleasure — and hopefully getting some decent shots in the process — by *unlearning* my ways. I'll have to resort to a queer

A juvenile unidentified starfish slowly crawls on the surface of a mound coral in shallow water, creating an image of arresting beauty in which the extreme simplicity of the subject greatly contrasts with the rich pattern of the starfish and its background. Rather than setting such scenes up - as it is often done by amateurs - one should instead strive to learn to actually recognize them when they present themselves.

example which might be of some use to a better understanding of this very Master Yoda-sounding concept. I happen to be a keen archer, and I particularly appreciate the style of archery which does away with modern, complex, carbon-fibre compound bows or sophisticated aiming devices. I like to use a traditional, simple yet powerful wooden take-down bow, and since I appreciate what is commonly known as instinctive archery I do not even take aim. Or, to be more precise, I do not align my arrow-tip and in fact I do not even look at it: I concentrate instead on the centre of the target and try to achieve that point of non-consciousness in which - as if magic but in fact only by finely-tuned instinct - my fingers will release the string and loose the arrow by themselves at exactly the "right" time, without a deliberate decision by my reasoning brain to do so, with my body marginally adjusting the aiming without actually making any sort of calculations. The trick consists in achieving this unencumbered by rational thinking – pull the string while raising the bow, look at the target, pause a second or two – without worrying if you're aiming right ! - and then loose the arrow. In the instant you loose it you'll know exactly if it's a good shot or not – almost as if you were guiding it towards its target by sheer willpower alone. If you did it right (or, better, if you did it all – there's no trying, only doing, to quote Master Yoda again) you'll experience the incredibly satisfying sensation of having achieved a miraculous balance – of having briefly been part of the flow of life. This may sound like

The ugly mug of the *Shrek*-like Giant jawfish *Opistognathus dendriticus*, a peaceful bottom-dwelling ogre of the deep endemic to the Sulu Sea, reveals a large clutch of almost ready-to-hatch eggs being lovingly brooded in its gaping mouth cavity. Careful observation in the field and previous, well-ingrained knowledge of one's subjects will often allow reaping rich rewards regarding previously undescribed behavior of marine species. With this image - taken a few years ago in Pulau Lankayan - we were the first ever to document oral brooding in this impressive species.

Guest
Photographer

Eric
CHENG

USA

Canon IDs MkII
Canon 180mm
Seacam housing
Ikelite DS125 dual strobes

A stroke of genius for Eric Cheng, who captures the coral reef of Papua New Guinea and a whole world reflected in a small air bubble trapped under a *Sarcophyton* soft coral - having stopped to truly see what is around him while his dive companions are probably complaining for a lack of subjects. Unfettered creativity, an absolute lack of fear of judgement and a very personal, unconventional approach to subjects are some of the most important ingredients requested by those truly interested in developing a personal expressive style - be it in photography or otherwise.

Guest
Photographer

Charles
HOOD
United Kingdom

Nikon D100
Nikon 28mm
Sea & Sea housing
ambient light

A powerful yet refined statement in symmetry, this face-on portrait of a Great hammerhead *Sphyrna mokarran* successfully contradicts the axiom of never shooting frontally - in this case, in fact, Charles Hood successfully captures the quintessence of the queer-looking pelagic predator framing it on a featureless deep blue background, its triangular, muscular shape radiating straight and curved lines - from its huge falcate dorsal fin to the scything pectorals, from the spectacular frontal lobes to the toothy grin of its arched mouth. Perfect shots such as this one are rare in the open ocean - apparently lucky, but in reality the perfect coincidence of several imponderable factors coming together and frozen in time by the photographer's instinctive reflex kicking in.

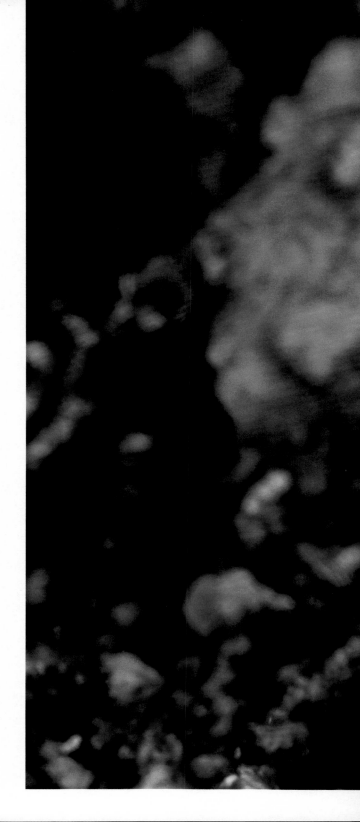

ridiculous mumbo-jumbo, but in fact my arrows strike the bull's eye quite often – much more than when I rationally concentrate on "calculated" aiming – and this state of semi-instinctive proficiency can be quite easily achieved by anybody with some open-minded experience and repeated practice. This – I hasten to add – is a school of archery practiced by many, and certainly not exclusive to me, whose roots can be traced to the discipline of *daishadokyo*, a mystical approach to *kyudo* or traditional Japanese archery. Back in the '50s and '60s the so-called hippie culture re-discovered a fascinating philosophical and yet very practical booklet, "*Zen and the Art of Archery*" by Eugen Herrigel (1948), which I strongly advise you to read and which explains how to follow this path immensely better than I could ever do. To quote from Wikipedia, "*a central idea in the book is that through years of practice, a physical activity becomes effortless both mentally and physically, as if the body executes complex and difficult movements without conscious control from the mind*". Herrigel's book, in any case, is also a hugely enjoyable read on its own merits, so go out and buy it.

At this point, it would not be wholly unreasonable in asking what rather obscure activities such as Zen and/or archery have in common with underwater photography. Everything, in my opinion. One, rediscovering and refining the instinctive reflex of shooting at exactly that perfect moment will give you immense satisfaction and the joy of hav-

The mating rituals of small, impossibly colorful Mandarin fish *Neosynchiropus splendidus* take place daily at twilight, over coral rubble bottoms in shallow water - the pair briefly rising in the water column in the fading light for a handful of precious, spectacular seconds, frantically ejecting eggs and sperm before falling back again and disappearing from sight. There is almost no time to consciously frame and focus in the subdued yellow shine of the lowered torch -only to act on impulse, following instict. This is one of the occasions in which digital has a distinctive advantage on film, not limiting the photographer to the customary 36 shots.

GUEST PHOTOGRAPHER

Guest
Photographer

John
SCARLETT
USA

Nikon D2X
Nikon 16mm fish-eye
Subal ND2 housing
ambient light

An exquisitely choreographed underwater ballet in which Tiger shark *Galeocerdo cuvier*, underwater photographers and the bow of the M/Y *Shearwater* - complete with onlookers - looming from above the surface blend in graceful harmony. John Scarlett freezes the action with perfect timing, framing his main subjects and the accessory ones - at least three more sharks in the background, two bursts of bubbles rising towards the surface - with an impeccable style in which, once more, instinct and technique blend to perfection.

Guest
Photographer

Jason
HELLER
USA

Nikon D200
Nikon 10.5mm fish-eye
Nexus housing
Sea & Sea YS 350 dual strobes

A good example of imaginative fish-eye composition, this essential yet striking image by Jason Heller is a colorful study in simplicity itself - impressionist underwater photography at its best. Shot at shallow depth in Wakatobi, Southern Sulawesi, Indonesia, it clearly demonstrates the spectacular visual results which can be achieved when correctly using fish-eyes for extreme close-ups. Notice how the green *Caulerpa* algae in the background subliminally act as an ideal bridge between the marine world and the land beyond.

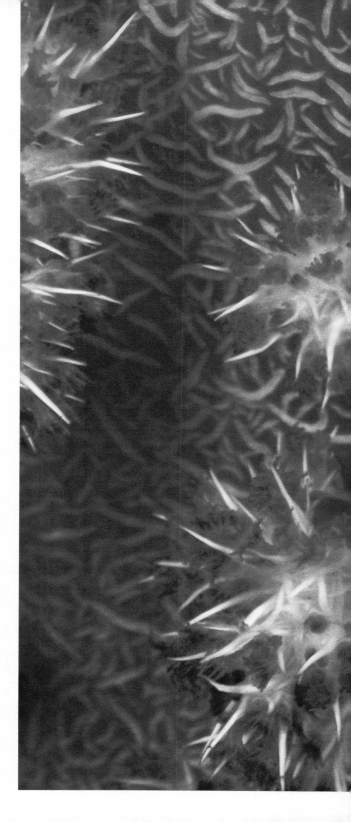

ing literally stilled time – which is what successful photography is all about. Two, it will make you a better photographer – as catching that elusive combination of subject, time and light is a matter of unreasoning instinct, not cold calculations (but more of this later – there are details to be discussed, and hopefully laboriously digested). Three, the rediscovery of your instincts will give you a better understanding of your deepest motivations, enriching your experiences as a diver and making a true sportsman out of you. Ah, sportsmanship – such an outdated term, isn't it? Who talks of sportsmanship anymore? Nowadays it's all about grabbing it all, quick and mindlessly, and guzzling it down in cheerless, hungry gulps. The availability of web space allows literally anybody to upload the fruits of their labour for everybody to see – which in turn fatally lowers the accepted standards. Think about it – up to a few years ago the only underwater photographs we'd see were those crisply printed on spectacular coffee-table books or glossy magazines. We'd see the cream of the crop only, the best of the best – carefully selected from hundreds of shots by hard-working professionals who'd spent days on end, if not weeks or months, to get them. *Those* were the examples we set ourselves to follow, to imitate, and to learn from. Nowadays it's the opposite – we're subject to an unstoppable avalanche of mediocrity, and this doesn't apply to underwater photography only, of course. This process numbs our senses and discernment, clouding our capacity to judge serenely and objectively.

Very young juvenile Pinnate batfish *Platax pinnatus* are much-sought and equally rare subjects, their orange-trimmed black livery and frantically sinuous swimming mode mimicking poisonous flatworms for defence from predators. Such subjects, when found - by trial or sheer luck -can and often will send the photographer in "sensory overload", provoking a lapse in concentration which usually results in wasted opportunities. Clear-minded focusing and a calm attitude will result in good results instead - care was taken in this instance to shoot only when the tiny fish was in front of the soft coral background, resulting in a forceful color statement.

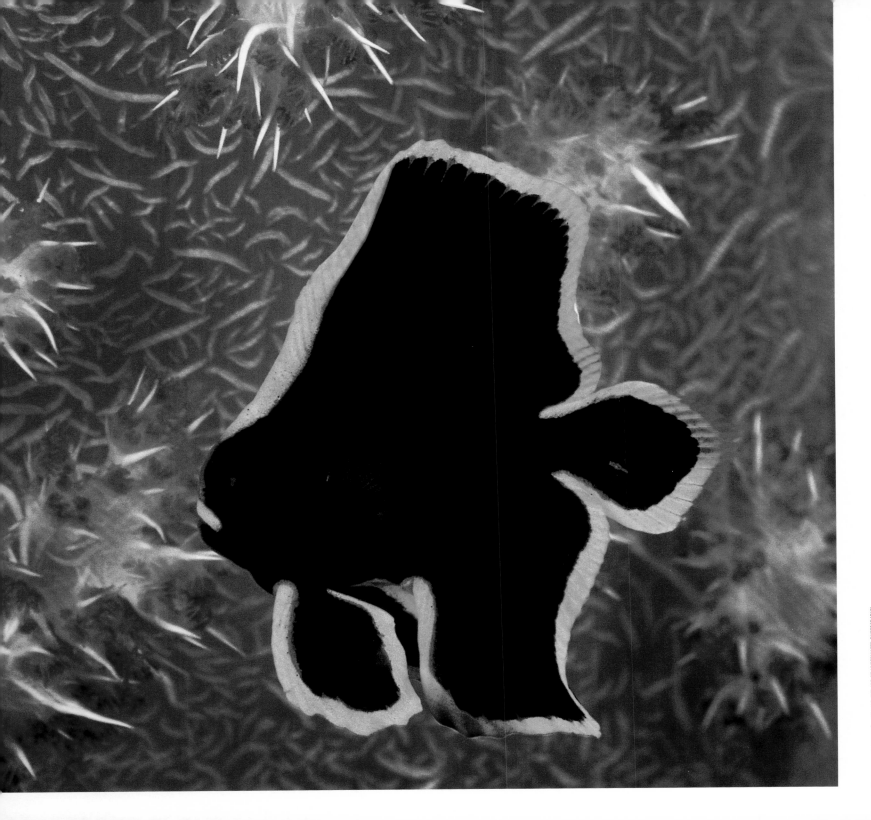

Guest
Photographer

Alex
MUSTARD
United Kingdom

Nikon D2X
Nikon 16mm fish-eye
Subal housing
2 Subtronic Alpha strobes

Not one shying away from "special effects", Alex Mustard adds a motion blur to this close-up fish-eye shot of a Flying gurnard *Dactyloptena orientalis*, making good use of the broad pectoral fins this species fans out when alarmed. Getting as close as possible to relatively small, approachable species with fish-eye lenses offers the possibility of obtaining visually arresting images, and adding a teleconverter to wide-angle ones even allows for unusual "wide-macro" shots. Such highly specialized experiments (and set-ups) are best left to experienced photographers who already have amassed a large number of more normal, readily usable shots of the same species, however, since they greatly restrict the underwater flexibility of the camera system once installed.

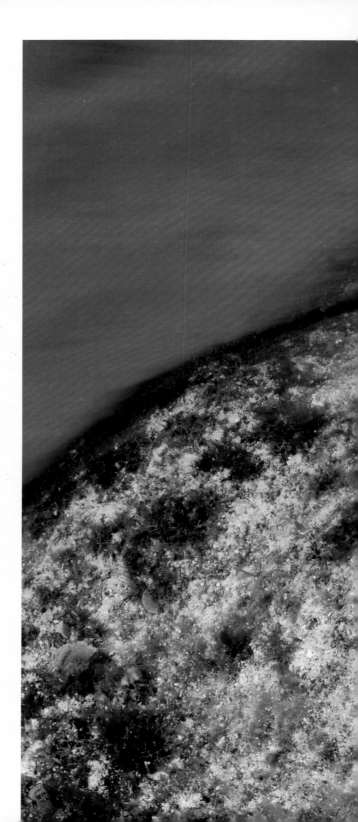

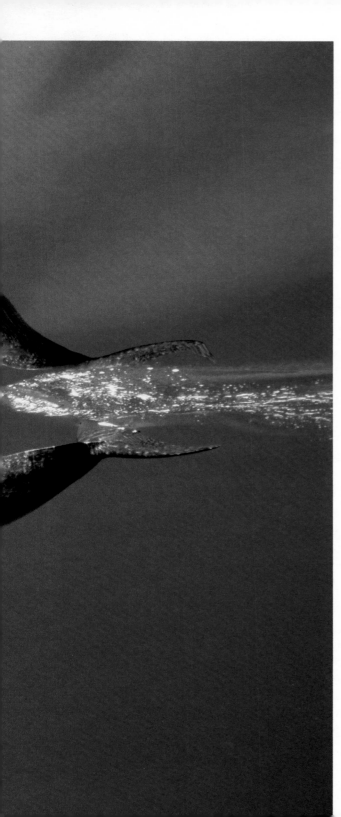

Guest
Photographer

Doug
PERRINE
USA

Nikonos V
Nikonos 15mm fish-eye
ambient light

Doug Perrine shows us what a true master can achieve - without even worrying for a second about the use of basic, technologically outdated equipment. Simple to the utmost and yet superbly balanced in all its components, this exquisite ballet of Atlantic spotted dolphins *Stenella frontalis* is almost hypnotic in its play on reflections - one truly has to pause and watch twice, before realizing there's only three of them. Taking full advantage with consummate ease of water and ambient light conditions and foreseeing by knowledge and experience his playful subjects' behavior, the author trascends here the medium to create a fully-fledged work of art, a time-frozen love declaration to the moving beauty of nature.

Quantity has little to do with quality. What about rediscovering the idea of sportsmanship then? I come from a time when every shot counted – we had only 36 in our roll of film. Only 36 bullets in our magazine, only 36 arrows in our quiver – and each one had to count. That's why we did our best to nail our target every time – because we didn't have much to spare. It was all part of the fun – if you missed your shot you just had to merrily curse yourself and shrug it off – it gave you a sense of perspective, and it greatly added to the satisfaction of having got it right when it happened. You and your subject were more or less on the same level, so to speak – you could stalk it, but it could outwit you, and the possibility of a big mistake was also always lurking around the corner. So many times I have metaphorically sportingly tipped my hat underwater to that clever fish which had escaped me ("*That was a jolly good game, old fellow – so long!*"). But the agony of those last three remaining frames in your camera was unbelievable – should I take them now with this uniquely colourful nudibranch, or should I wait for that unbelievable pod of pink tutu-wearing dolphins which will magically and unfailingly appear out of the blue during my safety stop at the end of the dive? Today, the advent of digital photography has given us an almost limitless supply of megabyte arrows instead – so a lot of people happily loose them all over the place, mindlessly firing them in to thin air, glibly wallowing in the dumb, empty satisfaction that everything will be easily fixed in Photoshop later on any-

We like to playfully call them the "Cartier shrimp", as these Ghost shrimp *Pliopontonia furtiva* slowly and deliberately tread the velvety surface of their corallimorpharian abode just like some precious brooches displayed in a jeweler's shop window - at least to our eyes. Even such elegant creatures, however, would result in uninteresting shots if photographed out of context: their beauty is exalted by the delicately nuanced, slightly textured surface they are usually observed on, a fleshy, rubbery tissue with a glassy appearance which perfectly compliments their yellow-accented transparent bodies.

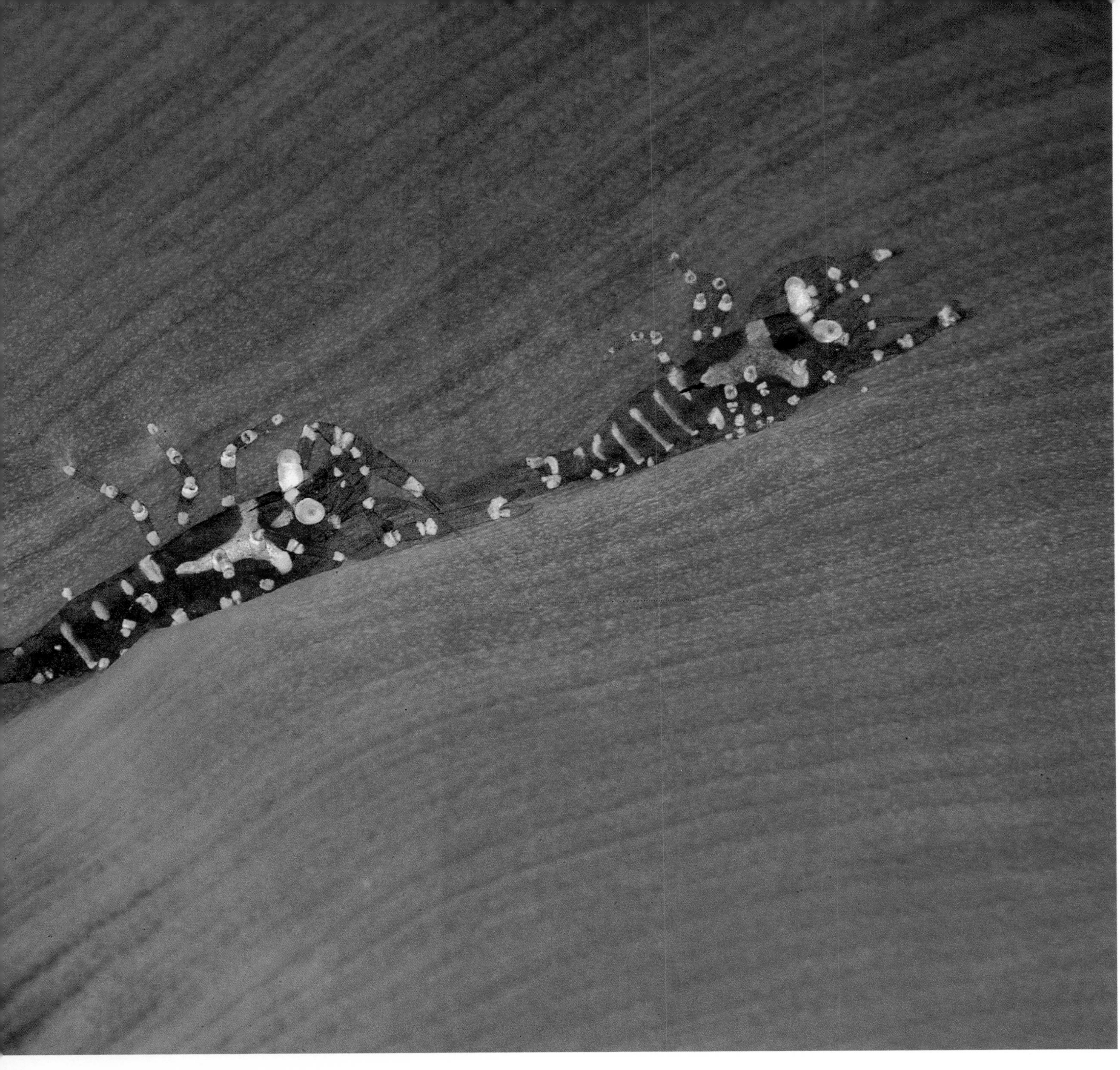

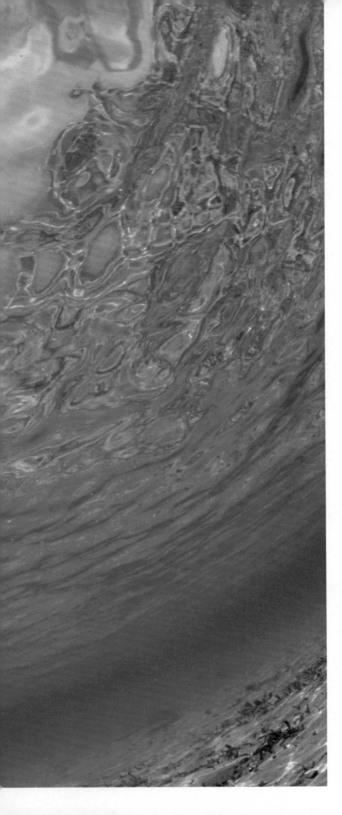

Doug
PERRINE

USA

Nikonos RS
Nikonos RS 13mm fish-eye
2 Ikelite Substrobe 200

Another masterful shot from Doug Perrine, this time of a notoriously wary subject which will seldom let divers approach this close: this beautiful Eagle ray *Aetobatis narinari* close-up portrait has been shot with a fish-eye lens, meaning that the subject was actually touching the dome port with the tip of its snout. Stalking shy subjects and learning to cross their path to surprise them at exactly the right time is in art in itself - not unlike old-time big game tracking and hunting - which one can only learn from direct experience in the field. Notice also how the perfectly framed and focused image makes good use of two optical properties characteristic of fish-eyes: the curved horizon and, most importantly, Snell's window, to register the clouds in the sky above the surface. The latter designates a more or less circular area through which above-water details become clearly visible when aiming fish-eye lenses directly towards the surface.

Guest
Photographer

Will
CHEN
USA

Canon 5D
Canon 16-35mm
Ikelite Housing
Ikelite DS125 dual strobes

The contrast between pure motion and eerie stillness has been caught to perfection by William Chen in this atmospheric shot of a Sea lion darting in an upward turn among the giant kelp of California's temperate shores at San Miguel Island. The dramatic yet strangely peaceful cathedral-like quality of this dreamy environment offers - with its greenish, stained-glass lighting - the ideal background to the sweeping motion of the streamlined mammal, frozen at the perfect apex of its turning motion. The dynamic tension of the Sea lion - perfectly positioned against the sun - offers an ideal, striking contrast to the immobility of the column-like kelp pillars among which it has been photographed, a testimony to the author's fast reflexes and creative vision.

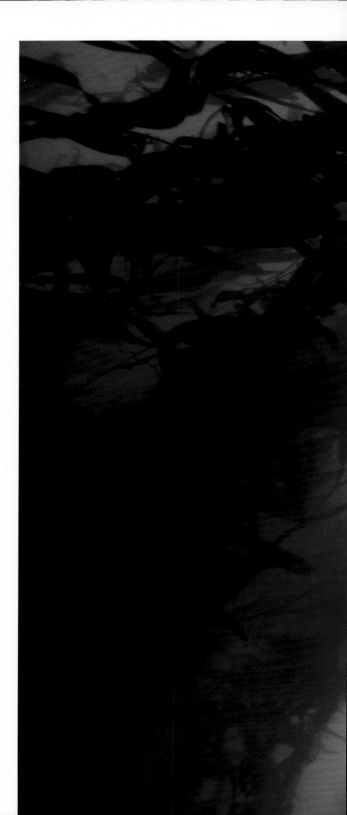

The occasional full side portrait - disparagingly referred to as "ID shot" by many - is in fact an excellent solution to be readily adopted in many instances: the fascinating Weedy filefish *Chaetoderma penicilligera* is so stubbornly convinced of the protection offered by its spectacular camouflage that it won't allow any approach from any other direction, constantly turning on its axis to offer its broad side to the photographer. It is a good occasion, then, to use the image to support a discussion about this species' interesting and rather unique behavior. Several marine species are so strange, weird and wonderful, in fact, that they do not necessitate any particularly creative effort by the photographer to produce exceptionally interesting images!

way. This is not how it should be done if we want to give it that real meaning which is so important to us as divers and photographers. We should instead try to get back to that sporting, chivalrous "one bullet, one shot" hunting philosophy which doesn't necessarily belong to a forgotten past, that discipline which will transform even the simple act of pressing the shutter trigger into an experience of creation, which will unexpectedly redefine the mundane into the extraordinary. To those who have never paused to give a thought to this way of acting, I can only say – do not dismiss it as a pseudo-philosophical meaningless babble, but look inside yourself and search for the answer. I am not saying that from now on you'll be allowed only one make-or-break click per subject, far from it. Nor I am saying this will magically transform your photographs in ready-made faultless works of art. Nothing can do that, except your own vision and genius. Simply enjoying concentration and achieving action in a flash without a conscious decision to act can, however, immensely enrich your photography skills, and above all regale you with the joy and satisfaction of finding yourself once more in harmonious balance with that endless, boundless world which surrounds you.

At this point I wouldn't be surprised, after all, if some of you were still unconvinced by all this, so I'll make it even simpler – remember the old saying "practice makes perfect"? It's just like that – just as the author-

Backgrounds are of the greatest importance in macrophotography, and one always has to be very alert and quick to take advantage of the good occasions when they present themselves. This jewel-like but deadly venomous Blue-ring octopus *Hapalochlaena lunulata* was spotted at twilight while resting in a perfect position on a brain coral in the Lembeh Strait. We immediately forgot the Mandarin fish we had come to shoot and spent our full dive with the tiny, pixie-like cephalopod, which we shot from every possible angle and in every possible livery. Yet, to my eyes the best image is still the first one, in which the raised skin flaps of the octopus and the geometric pattern of the coral surface texture ideally blend into an image of beauty.

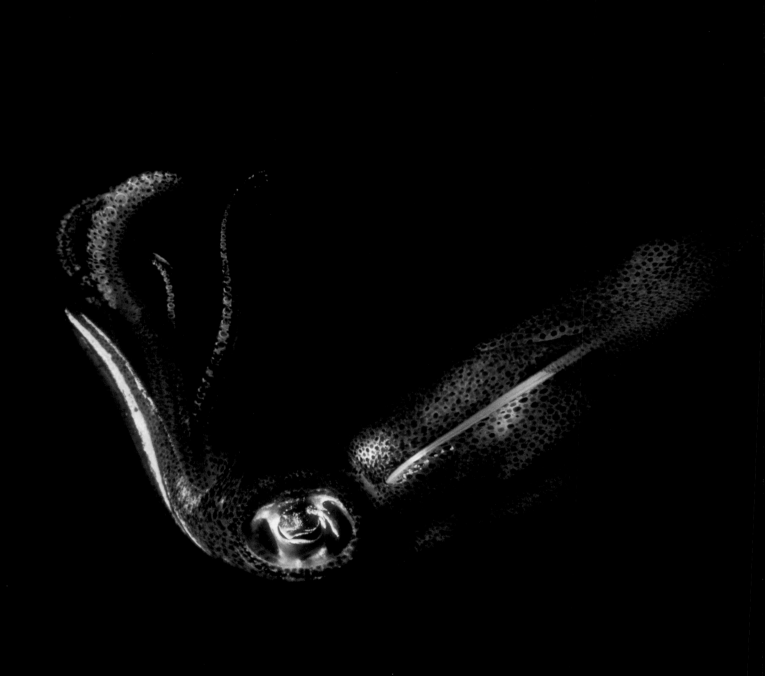

Guest
Photographer

Stephen
WONG

Hong Kong

Nikon F801s
Nikon105mm
Ikelite housing
Ikelite 225 + Nikonos SB103 strobes

Open water night time photography requires a great deal of coordination and well-established routines, as everything around the photographer is cloaked in the densest darkness - sense of direction and movement are often impaired. Stephen Wong has perfectly captured the mystery and mystique of nocturnal underwater camerawork with this side portrait of a Bigfin reef squid *Sepioteuthis lessoniana* - a roving, intelligent predator which at night flashes mysterious signals from its light-emitting chromatophores. Its motion a statement in elegance - its long front tentacles raised, as in a mysterious offering to an underwater deity - the squid has deliberately been underexposed to evidence its magical bioluminescence, which would have otherwise been washed out by the strobes at full power.

GUEST PHOTOGRAPHER

Responsible underwater photographers should strictly refrain from artificially posing their marine subjects, moving them around or grouping them together in the false hope of a better shot. It is incredibly more satisfying - and usually more fruitful - taking immediate advantage of any good chance when it presents itself, as it happened with these three neatly tiered Ornate ghostpipefish *Solenostomus paradoxus* when they paraded for us in the murky waters of the Lembeh Strait. It does not take long to learn to anticipate the behavior of most small marine animals once one takes the trouble to actually stop and observe them for a while.

pupil of "*Zen and the Art of Archery*" was requested by his enigmatical teacher to endlessly repeat an apparently meaningless series of gestures and ritualistic positions before being even allowed to loose his first arrow, so you will have to thoroughly familiarize yourself with the dials, knobs and inner workings of your camera, to absorb influences of styles and images from other media (even unexpected ones, as we'll see later), to practice to perfection your diving and buoyancy skills, to learn whatever you are willing to learn about the marine life surrounding you... until all these matters will have been fully embraced. If you can absorb knowledge and make it become one with you, that same acquired knowledge will unerringly and instantaneously flow from you instinctively when needed, and you will finally be able to forget yourself and be the part of the whole. This should make a better underwater photographer out of you – and if it doesn't, well, you'll have learned something good anyway.

A study in mischievous impudence, this portrait of a tiny Bartel's dragonet *Neosynchiropus bartelsi* makes good use of the impish looks and puckered mouth of these exceptionally colorful little fish, occasionally observed hopping around on coral rubble bottoms at shallow depth. Always on the move, seldom pausing for the photographer, these subjects require good camera control and quick reflexes since depth of field is absolutely minimal due to their small size. The substrate they are found on often offers interesting contrasting patterns, as in the case illustrated here.

Chapter 3

FRAMING AND LIGHTING
Great photos are everywhere, you just have to take them

- Principles of instinctive composition
- Learning from movies
- Use of strobes
- Taking advantage of natural light
- Why TTL is so important for you
- Focus, don't fidget!
- Learn to know your subjects
- Read, read, read!
- The perils of post-production

There is no such thing as perfectly framing an underwater picture in my opinion – but there are several ways of framing it wrong. It seems such a pity seeing how so many lucky people, who can afford to travel to distant lands and use expensive camera equipment, can throw away wonderful photo opportunities. Either, because they never care to stop and think for a second or never learned the basics before getting into the water... and believe me, I have seen this happening quite often. Fish looking the wrong way (i.e. away from the viewer) or miss-

A good example of a well-framed image, which has several times been subsequently published as an opening double spread on books and dive magazines thanks to its engaging distribution of colors and masses. All the necessary elements coalesce here to success: a reasonably structured but not overwhelming background, two colorful, contrasting subjects close to each other and pointing in the right direction - ie towards the empty space on their opposite side - while emerging from a dark background, a slice of blue sea in the opposite corner. Not really difficult from a technical point of view, composing shots such as this one requests however a well-developed feeling for perspective and lighting.

ing a tail, photos taken from above or from the side when the opposite should have happened, beautiful subjects marred by insignificant backgrounds, wide-angle reef shots marred by ridiculous divers flapping wildly and clumsily in the background, great pictures ruined by wrong lighting...the list is endless. And I bet these same people would never do the same basic mistakes if they were taking photographs on land – they'd be fastidious and ridiculously obsessive with their subject, camera and light placement. So what is their problem? Bluntly put, their diving skills are woefully inadequate. So, lesson number one – you'll never be able to take good photos underwater if you don't feel perfectly at home while diving. Some lucky people are born with an innate aquatic affinity, others have to learn the skills, but the bottom line is that to be a good underwater photographer you must be able to behave in the sea exactly as if you were on land, i.e. not being distracted or, even worse, actually worried by your breathing rhythm, your buoyancy problems, the equipment you're wearing, what you had for breakfast. You must be aware but not concerned about where you are, be it a raging current or quiet muck – you must feel perfectly comfortable and be able to really enjoy what you're doing. Antonella and I often chat to each other while underwater – I just take my regulator out and talk, and she claims she can hear my words popping out of the air bubbles! That's what I mean by being comfortable. Once you feel ok and are having fun, start looking around for a subject – and when

Close-up shots can often achieve interesting results, as in this face-on portrait of a Crocodile fish *Cymbacephalus beauforti* taken in Malaysia. The complex Oriental rug-like patterns of its camouflaged livery, the branched eye flaps and the colorful reflections from the two strobes' flash would not produce the same striking effect, however, if the subject had been framed from a different position. Full frontal shots are quite tricky with expressionless subjects, but their occasional anthropomorphisizing of fish - giving them smiles, scowls and pouting lips - is often appreciated by non-divers. Static subjects such as these fish offer excellent opportunities to practice the art of extreme close-up.

you've found one, stop for a second and think (we're still talking about essentially static subjects here — you're not expected to pause and ponder if a mako shark is whizzing by! More of this later). Try to visualize the shot you'd like to create — is the sun positioned right? Is anything in the foreground which might spoil the photo? Is there anything in the background which might look wrong? Is there a way for you to enhance the shot — like waiting for a particular fish to position itself in a certain spot, or asking your buddy to enter the frame? These are simple basic questions, and yet a great many inexperienced underwater photographers do not stop to ponder them at all. Decently framing your subject is also inextricably linked to the kind of lens you're using at the moment

The use of fish-eye lenses offers exciting opportunities when diving on rich, healthy coral reefs in good visibility. This image - taken on the Liberty wreck in Tulamben, Bali - shows the correct positioning of the model in the background, gracefully posed against the sunburst, and a vibrant, colorful environment. Note the slight deformation of the image at the corners of the image, typical of close-up work with fish-eyes.

— macro and wide angle are obviously not the same (even if one could arguably take incredible "wide-macro" shots with a teleconverter added to a fish-eye). Having reached the point where you feel totally comfortable underwater and are automatically asking you these simple basic questions without even realizing it, represents the first step in the right direction - but this will be useless without the next one. The question we have to ask ourselves now, is — by what parameters can a photograph be defined as "correctly framed"? Well, a correctly framed photo might attract the attention of the viewer to an interesting and otherwise obscure detail of the subject; or clearly show the subject in its well-defined entirety; or convey impressions of light and motion

Another good example of fish-eye composition, this time taken in the exceptionally beautiful setting of Five Rocks in Raja Ampat, West Papua. Notice the sun rays streaming from the cavern-like opening at the top - through which trees and clouds can actually be observed - and the carefully timed shooting to correctly position the stream of exhaled bubbles. In this instance composition makes good use of the dramatic, theatrical quality of the environment.

through the use of photographic techniques, such as a slow shutter speed; it might convey the idea of power, or menace, fragility, or elegance depending on the subject – and so on. All these variations – and endless more – are entirely dependent on the composition of your shot, on how you are looking at your subject, by its relative position to you and by the lighting employed, be it strobes or natural light. With experience - and learning from our mistakes - we can teach ourselves to continuously improve, attaining the point when we'll more or less correctly frame our subject by reflex or, if you prefer, by the Zen-like instinct mentioned in the previous chapter (and this is when you are ready not to pause when that mako shark whizzes by again). Again, practice makes perfect – but practice must be accompanied by the humility to recognize our own errors and by the willingness to learn from them.

Properly composing a shot is a difficult art that can make or break your photo . Often it is just a slight but critical creative difference in composition and lighting, an effort of imagination, which will make an image stand out in a crowd of otherwise good but average shots, making it a work of art. Not easy to achieve and often impossible for most of us – so let's be satisfied with getting ourselves a "good" shot for a start! Start by avoiding the silly, simple little horrors I mentioned above, and then start looking at photos you like and admire – and try

It would have been preferable to have the subject - a brilliantly colored Coral cod *Cephalopholis miniata* - to be slightly more offset to the left, but very often the photographer has little choice. This image - shot on a late afternoon in the Red Sea - shows to good effect the feeling of depth which can be achieved by shooting subjects in perspective and along diagonal lines, particularly when they are emerging from dark recesses and shadowy areas. The correct positioning of strobes is very important in such instances, as it is all too easy to have the light aimed at the subject bounced back by some unforeseen overhanging coral or rock. Any healthy, undisturbed coral reef will normally offer a large number of opportunities such as this in the course of a dive to observing, slow-moving photographers.

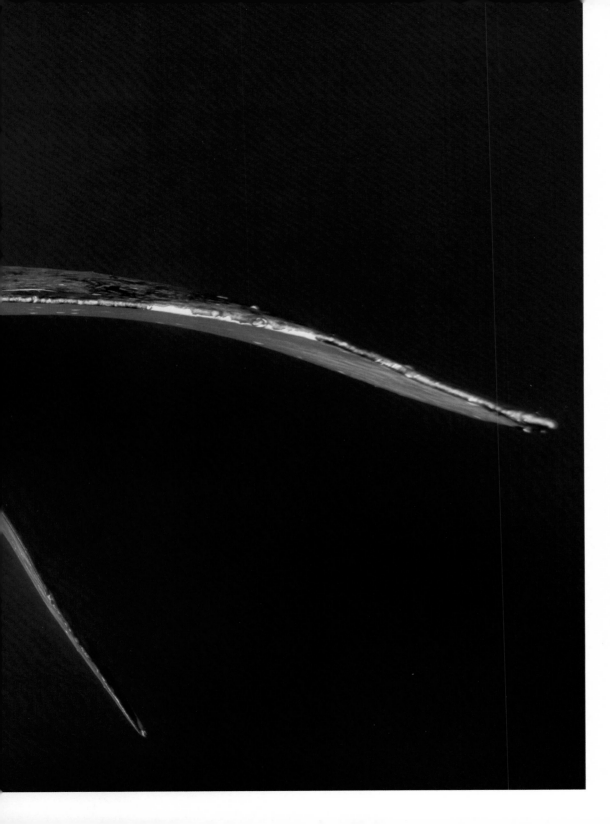

Guest
Photographer

Tony
WU

Japan

Canon 5D
Canon 20mm
Zillion housing
ambient light

Rules can be occasionally bent - when one is however strictly following others and testing creativity. In his search for the perfect whale image, Tony Wu creates a beautiful, unexpected image of symmetry by going against the rules and shooting this diving Humpback *Megaptera novaeangliae* from the back, at the same time achieving an extraordinarily difficult, perfectly geometrical composition. The result is a love declaration in Chinese calligraphy to the sea and its mysterious, wandering giants.

to emulate them, not as a final objective, but as a basic training to achieve your own results, to develop your own creativity. For example, it doesn't take much to learn by imitation how to correctly position sunbursts in a corner of the frame to achieve pleasing results – if that effect is the one you're looking for – but it makes such a pleasing difference when you have learned to do it properly. Once you've taught yourself that little discipline needed not to cut a fish's head or tail off, you should begin to experiment a little more with perspective and the positioning of your subject within the frame of the photo. Now think about this – great movie sequences seldom put their subject squarely in the middle of the set. Teachers of the old-school will tell you to study great paintings to learn about this, but movies are more accessible and usually more easily understood. If a film director wants to convey a sense of loneliness or danger, he'll frame his player in a corner, often from above, with a lot of space surrounding the subject – space which isolates and at the same time traps the cowering character. Do that with a marine creature – like a turtle - swimming by itself in the empty blue and you'll powerfully and immediately increase the viewer's perception of the surrounding ocean's immensity.   But if you employ the same solution framing your subject from a point below the spectator's eye-line, the effect will be quite the opposite – it'll be a towering figure of power and even menace, a figure conveying superhuman strength. Boris Karloff as the Frankenstein monster and

Reef canyons, deep wall cracks and shadowy crevices can often be used to obtain spectacular results in composition. This colorful, dynamic image - published in print several times, once as the cover to a Red Sea dive guide - was taken in a weak current and from a low vantage point at Panorama Reef. Notice how the dark background is interrupted by a slice of bright blue sea at the top - which adds visual interest and depth - and how the sharp strobe lighting from the sides adds to the texture and movement of the giant anemone and its attending clownfish. The slightly distorted and out-of-focus corner areas of the photo are an unwelcome but unavoidable optical effect when using fish-eyes, and can often be cropped out in publishing.

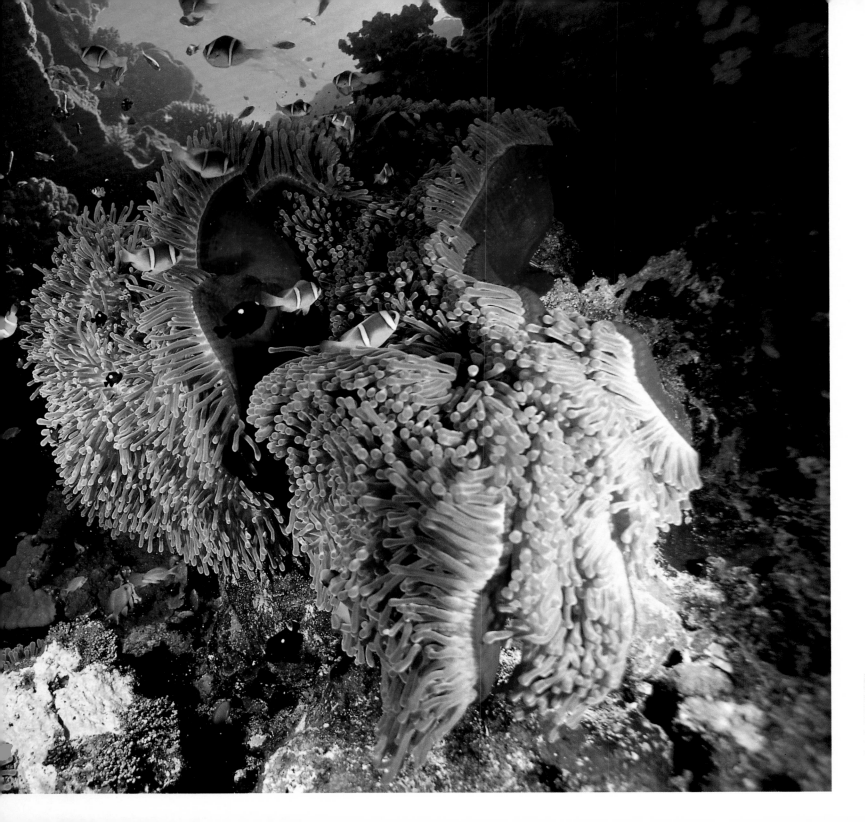

Guest
Photographer

Will
CHEN
USA

Canon 5D
Sigma 50mm
Ikelite housing
Ikelite DS125dual strobes

A simple but mesmerizing study in chromatic contrast and brilliant composition, this sharp portrait of a Garibaldi against the surface was created by William Chen while diving at San Clemente Island, California. The blue mirroring surface at shallow depth regales to the image a distinct painting-like quality, and the Impressionist feeling is strongly enhanced by the bright orange fish, off-set and isolated on the azure background. Notice also how the crisscrossing silvery secondary subjects in the background enrich the composition, adding a slight feeling of movement and depth to an otherwise dreamily static image. A brilliant - in all senses! - photograph showing to perfection the concept of instinctive response applied to underwater photography.

Guest
Photographer

Roger
HORROCKS

South Africa

Nikon D200
Nikon 10.5mm fish-eye
Sea & Sea housing
ambient light

South African Roger Horrocks adds his distinct, unmistakable personal and slightly "Gothic" touch to this atmospheric shot of a Green turtle *Chelonia mydas* diving in the surge to escape the rain. Often taking his images while freediving in the open ocean, occasionally among large, fast and potentially dangerous subjects, the author has little use for cumbersome strobes, relying on superb physical condition and available ambient light to achieve his evocative photographic results. Underwater photography of this kind trascends technology, transforming itself into a highly spiritual exercise in which the cult of the physical body and that of the purely instinctual mind blend to perfection.

Acting on pure reflex, Roger Horrocks achieves in this image the same sense of isolation carefully planned by celebrated movie director Fritz Lang when filming this chase scene for his masterpiece *M*. German Expressionist movies of the '20s and '30s represent extraordinary tutorials to learn the art of framing.

machine-gun toting gangsters in the '30s were always filmed like this! That's why a frontal or three-quarter shot of a shark coming towards you will look best when framed from slightly below – you'll be able to show to advantage its weighty mass, its toothy grin and its blade-like pectoral fins. If instead you want to convey the sense of incredible elegance and sinuous beauty, rather then menace, conveyed by the same animal try to photograph it from above a blue water or white sand background, and be prepared to be surprised by the enormous difference in perception. Framing a coral reef from below, rising up like a cliff from the depths with the surface and a sunburst in the background, will give it a sense of mass and shadowy mystery (as some parts of the image will be naturally backlit) for the reasons mentioned above, but an image of that same reef taken from above in natural light will instead, instantly communicate the feeling of a serene tropical heaven. Again, filming a crowd in its entirety from far away will convey the sense of a seething mass and of mindless movement. Think of the bird's eye views of the battlefields of every war movie from *All Quiet on the Western Front* to *Saving Private Ryan* and the *Lord of the Rings* trilogy and you should clearly comprehend my meaning. So, you might want to frame a twirling tornado of jacks suspended in open water in the same way to get an image of massed silvery reflections, of powerful action, even of elegant suspended motion. But get close to the action itself – pushing your camera down, so to speak, at ground level in the dust of

A Grey reef shark *Carcharhynus amblyrynchos* patrols the reef of Layang Layang in the South China Sea at dawn. The evocative use of back-lit images shot at available ambient light has been pionereed by the movie industry in the '20s and '30s, as shown in this frame from Eizenstein's *Alexander Nevsky*.
The same technique can be used today by underwater photographers to add emotional nuances to their images or to take advantage of situations in which artificial illumination by strobes would be otherwise difficult or impossible.

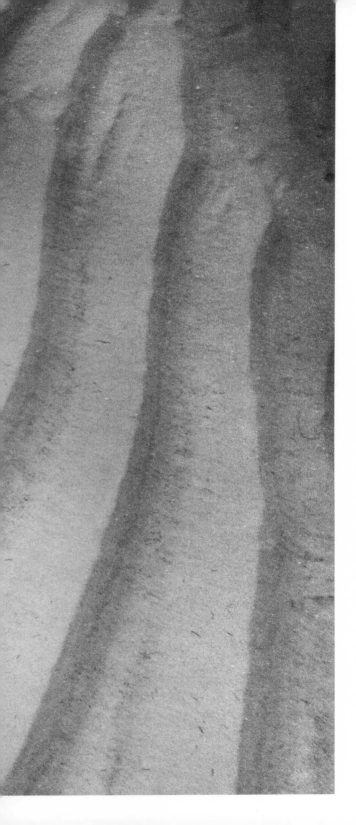

Guest
Photographer

Alex
MUSTARD

United Kingdom

Nikon D2X
Nikon 12-24mm
Subal housing
ambient light

A Caribbean reef shark *Carcharhynus perezi* gracefully patrols the sandy seabottom of the Bahamas. A quiet photographic statement of refined elegance, this imaginative shot by Alex Mustard dispenses with the common image of the shark as a powerful, dangerous predator, choosing instead to pay homage to is exquisite, seductive beauty. The slow, sinuous motion of the shark - here reduced to little more than a dark silhouette - is exalted by its brilliant juxtapositioning on the equally wavy but perpendicular wave markings on the sandy bottom, and the stark monochromatic contrast between the two elements is further stated by the choice of black and white.

battle, among the fighting, the shooting and the blood – and you'll find yourself immersed in the drama of the single soldiers, one falling wounded here, another rising victorious there. Do that with a packed school of barracudas –silently slinking inside the spiralling mass to get really close – and your images will suddenly now bring to life the steely crazy glare, the white jutting fangs, the chrome-plated reflective scales of the big toothy predators, now incredibly full of personality. Seeing a lot of old classic movies from the '30s, '40s and '50s – a period during which films were much more creatively crafted than today - is a very enjoyable and useful way to learn about the secrets of framing and its uncanny ability to convey a spectacular sense of drama by the position-ing of the camera alone. Like many movie-makers of the past, you'll also rapidly learn to use perspective to add another dramatic dimen-sion to your images – having another, smaller and secondary subject in the frame (let's say your backlit buddy) will add a sense of proportion and possibly dramatic balance otherwise missing from your photo-graph. Think of the difference such a secondary subject can make in the image of a whale shark, for example! Once you feel more assured of yourself you might also want to experiment with less conventional framing to obtain unexpected effects – a difficult but spectacular trick is shooting upwards close to the surface, especially in very flat seas, to obtain the incredibly pleasing effects of reflection (of the subject itself, which can actually be fully mirrored, especially at night) or conversely

Backlit reef faces and walls always offer an image of mystery and dark mass, in this instance exalted by several correctly positioned secondary elements: the diver, the brightly colored parrotfish adding a counterpoint at the lower left, the teeming masses of basslets everywhere. A great tutorial in the dynamic, architectural use of milling crowds and building structures is of course Fritz Lang's legendary science fiction movie *Metropolis*.

of the actual transparency (with bright white clouds and even coastal vegetation clearly visible in the background). Opportunities are literally endless and limited only by your own imagination and creativity, as long as you remember a few basic rules:

One, always have your subject looking at you or at least in your general direction and always focus on the eye.

Two, do not cut any part of the subject out of the frame.

Three, restrict shots from directly above for only creative effects (or identification photos of flounders!).

Four, remember that while same-level full-side images of marine life are the best for identification purposes, full frontal or three-quarter

A swirling, tornado-like milling school of Bigeye jacks *Caranx sexfasciatus* at the world-famous drop-off of Sipadan, Borneo. Carefully framed from straight below - taking care not to exhale any bubbles! - along the diagonal separation between the dark reef wall and the brightly lit sky above, this image has been published in print several times, being also chosen as the cover of our book *Borneo - an Underwater Paradise*.

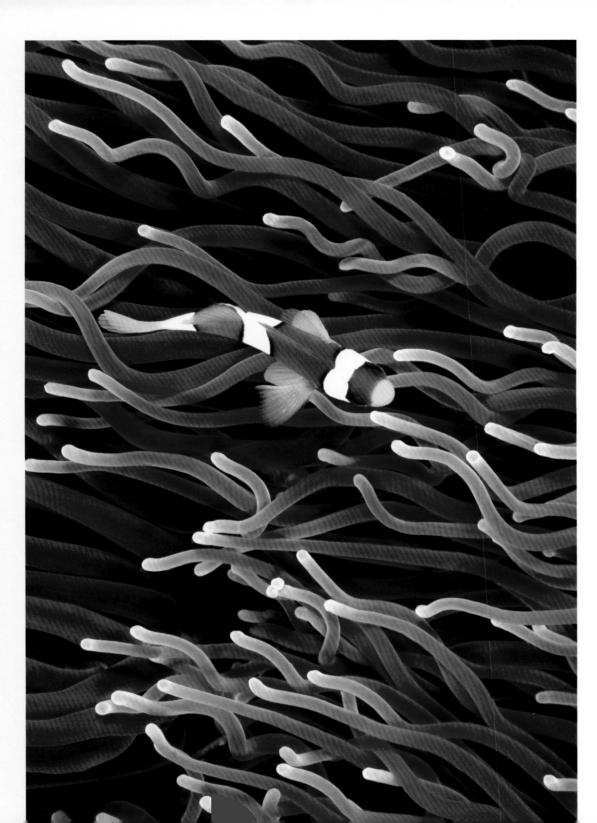

Alex
MUSTARD

United Kingdom

Nikon D100
Nikon 105mm
Subal housing
2 Subtronic Alpha strobes

A joyful, colorful play on undulating motion, this imaginative shot by Alex Mustard goes against the book - shooting from straight above and painting at the same time a sharply contrasting tapestry, in which the banded livery and the sinuous motion of the juvenile clownfish are faultlessly juxtaposed on the swaying purple-pink tentacles of its anemone. How many times the same identical situation has been observed by underwater photographers - without being actually *seen*?

shots will add a lot of personality and appeal to your subjects.

Five, off-set subjects are always more interesting than dead-centred ones.

Six, diagonal lines are always more appealing than horizontal ones, i.e. try to shoot in perspective rather than on flat planes.

Each reasonably good photographer eventually develops their own style of framing, depending on the results to be achieved, and that usually will be one of one of the strongest characteristics of their photography.

But – you hoped it would be this easy, didn't you? This is only half of the story, as another incredibly powerful tool of the photography is the use of light itself (the term photography actually means "*writing / painting with light*"). As any topside wildlife photographer, you'll be able to choose between artificial and natural light (or carefully mix the two), and as any topside landscape photographer you'll have to resort to the use of available ambient light alone, as the scope of your subject – be it a coral reef or a grassy prairie – will defeat the power and range of any flash gun. As all divers know, colours are gradually absorbed as we get deeper, with reds being the first to disappear (looking like browns

The shimmering, steely phalanx of Chevron barracudas *Sphyraena qenie* parading at full strength by Layang Layang's reef in the South China Sea offers a fearsome spectacle of massed predatory efficiency. At this distance strobes can be safely used at full power on such highly reflective subjects to add some light accents. Once more, an excellent tutorial in the photographic use of tightly-knit orchestrated masses is offered by Eizenstein's propaganda classic *Alexander Nevsky*.

and blacks to our eyes), so the use of strobes will be imperative starting just a few feet under the surface if we want to render the colours of our subjects in their natural, dazzling glory (recent scientific research indicates however that reef fishes colour perception is actually quite at variance to ours, with these animals being very sensitive to ultraviolet frequencies and appearing to each other in dramatically different livery than they do to us – so much for objective portrayals of reality!). As with topside wildlife photography, the first result you want to obtain is that of giving your image a naturalistic look, bringing out the colours without the obvious use of the strobes' artificial light. This is where most inexperienced underwater photographers stumble, especially since the advent of digital cameras. First of all, natural ambient light comes generally from all sides and mostly from above – so we want to achieve a soft, even illumination and avoid harsh, strong shadows, as they will look most unnatural underwater. This means that the use of two strobes, one from each side, is imperative to get professional-looking results – each one carefully positioned at a 45° angle towards the subject, kept more or less slightly above the horizontal (adapt to your personal liking by judging the results) and close to the lens (for macro) or as far as possible from it (for wide angle and fish-eye shots) by the closely monitored positioning of your strobe arms. I stress "closely monitored positioning" as I've witnessed too many times fellow photographers – even rather experienced ones - diving

Closing in on the highly reflective barracudas, expressive close-ups of their toothy grin and crazed, staring eyes will now require a careful use of strobes to avoid overexposing. In such instances TTL readings can be misleading, so it is advisable to underexpose by one-half to one full f-stop. The emotional power of close-ups is well exemplified by the mad, man-hunting Count Zaroff in Schoedsack's fast-paced *The Most Dangerous Game*.

Guest
Photographer

Doug
PERRINE
USA

Canon Eos D60
Canon 15mm fish-eye
UK-Germany housing
Inon Z220dual strobes
polecam

Bending the rules once more - and achieving extraordinary success doing so - Doug Perrine's pair of Tiger sharks *Galeocerdo cuvier* sneak in from the frame's edge, side by side, the one in the background mischievously rolling its big round eye at the toothy grin of its companion in the foreground. Both exceptionally expressive, they are lords of the deep, dark sea in this moody shot taken at the Protea Banks off the Natal coast in South Africa. A high aperture setting darkens the background, giving a golden glow to the sun's rays slanting down and adding to the atmospheric feel of this wonderful image. To obtain it, the author utilized a polecam - a remotely-controlled camera affixed to a pole, which is lowered in the water from a boat when subjects are too dangerous or too wary to let photographers come close.

Guest
Photographer

Doug
SLOSS
USA

Nikonos V
Nikonos 15mm fish-eye
Nikon SB103 dual strobes

Blocking the sun behind, and while doing so allowing the foliage of the Rock Islands and the hull of the dive boat above to be discernible to the viewer, flaring its spectacular pectoral, ventral and dorsal venomous fins like a crazed samurai, Doug Sloss' beautiful Lionfish *Pterois volitans* is a text-book example of brilliant framing and lighting. A fitting example for the digital generation, showing what can be achieved with the right lens and a basic, outdated camera system when active creativity is at work.

Ketrick
CHIN
Malaysia

Nikon D2X
Nikon 16mm fish-eye
Nexus housing
Inon Z220S dual strobes

A simpler but no less effective approach for a less showy species, the streamlined, surface-dwelling (and very difficult to approach) Crocodilefish *Tylosurus crocodilus*. Shooting against the surface at Kapalai, in Malaysian Borneo, Ketrick Chin expertly positions his subject in a steep diagonal against the curving background, using the bright sky above - and a portion of the dive resort's wooden walkways - to fill an otherwise empty frame. The end result perfectly captures the sleek, missile-like lines of this fast surface predator.

Fiona
AYERST
South Africa

Nikon D200
Nikon 105mm
Sea & Sea housing
Sea & Sea YS120 dual strobes

Radically cropped here for publication - in the proportions of this layout, the black background of the original image would occupy the full two-page spread - this highly unusual image of a swimming Bobtail squid *Euriprymna* sp by Fiona Ayerst is a very

GUEST PHOTOGRAPHER

good example of how useful in editorial use and general publishing some off-the-beaten-track shots can be. At first sight, the original image appears to be quite out of balance, with its adorable, tiny squid-from-outer-space subject floating all alone on the far right of the inky black background; but by judicious use of cropping this same image can be readily transformed in a striking, unique horizontal layout - a perfect two-page spread introducing a magazine article, or a good advertising background. The lesson here? Think twice before destroying images in which the subject appears to be too small or too offset - as long as it is in sharp focus and of some interest, the extra neutral background might come in handy at a cropping stage later, allowing graphic designers and magazine editors to insert copy at leisure.

with incredibly expensive rigs only to spend most of their dive and their shooting with both strobes aimed anywhere but their subject. Even if carefully positioned at the start of the dive, it will often happen that one or both strobes will be knocked or pushed around, so always keep on checking the actual position of the flash head in relation to the subject before you shoot, and do not be afraid to reposition them constantly to obtain the effect you're looking for. This is one of the "fighter pilot" routines we'll discuss in detail further on in a later chapter. To add some subtle interest to your image – especially when doing macro photography – you might also want to employ one diffuser on one of the strobes, it doesn't matter which one, to obtain softer shad-

Superbly camouflaged, most Frogfish species make wonderful subjects for dramatic close-ups, allowing photographers unusual angles and perspectives. Three-quarter or even sideways portraits on a neutral or possibly black background will abruptly reveal undreamed of skin textures and colors, often invisible to the naked eye underwater.

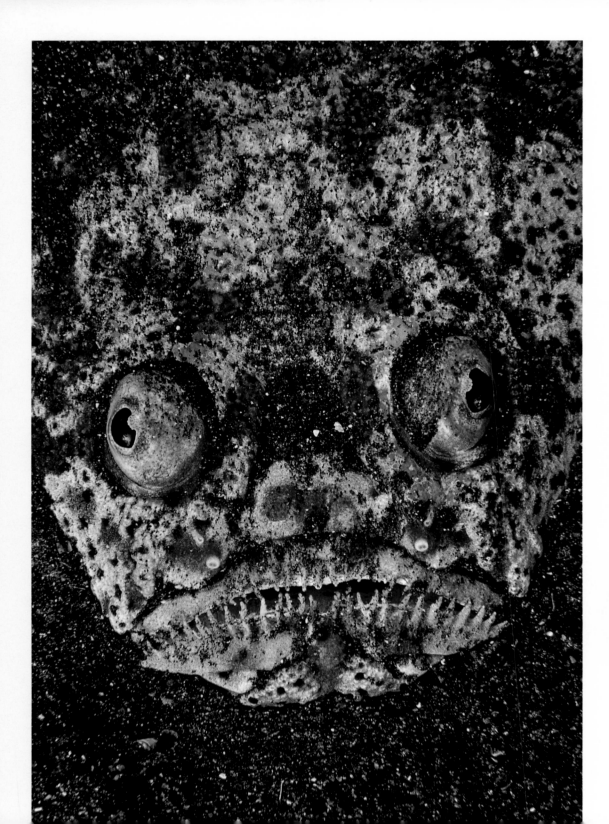

ows on one side of your subject (always remember – absolute symmetry doesn't look natural!). The trick is avoiding in any case full-frontal lighting, which will flatten your subjects and transform properly framed images in unappealing mug shots.

The correct amount of artificial light and its measurement has always been another long-standing object of heated discussion in underwater photography circles – manual or TTL? Human (read "*artful*" and "*creative*") or automated (read "*unthinking*" or "*idiotic*") judgement? I've seen this happen too many times in the past to enter the fray again – twenty years ago, when TTL first became available to underwater photographers, voices were raised in a chorus by the old

Movie buffs will immediately recognize in the *Uranoscopus sulphureus* Stargazer's glare the same mad intensity shown by the unforgettable robot of Fritz Lang's *Metropolis*. Film masterpieces are an unbeatable source of inspiration for underwater photography.

grizzled hands, the traditionalist divers who wouldn't accept it, immediately tagging it as "stupid" and "unreliable", swearing by their old (and quite often very fallacious) manual theories. Why, you weren't a real photographer if you used such gadgets! TTL new users, unbiased by tradition and listening to their own logic, took the world of underwater photography by storm, sweeping aside most of the old stubborn guys in a few years. With the advent of digital photography I've seen the same tidal wave coming back — everybody started enthusiastically congratulating themselves about the amount of time they would spend underwater checking their histograms rather than looking at fish and generally enjoying the dive. Bad picture? No problem, pal — just check your histogram, fumble around and take another one! Wrong again? Ooops — re-check your histogram and repeat! Ok, enough ranting — I'm all the way for TTL, obviously. All the pictures taken by us in this book were taken in TTL — all of them. The most tampering I've done — once in a million — is the occasional slight underexposing with very reflective subjects, like barracudas or jacks, when a little personal judgement is clearly needed. TTL is just a tool, but an incredibly evolved and useful one — it will let you concentrate on your subject, on framing, on the composition of the image, rather than have you worrying about exposure, fumbling with buttons, looking at histograms and quite possibly losing your subject — which, being probably a fish, won't be very interested in sitting around waiting for you to make up

Always try to put to good use strongly contrasting patterns and colors when setting up your shot - here a Longnose hawkfish *Oxycirrhites typus* shows off its tartan-like disruptive camouflage among the branching gorgonian colony it lives on. Gaudy and colorful once lit by the strobes' powerful flash, the scene looks however a muted maze of dark browns and blacks to the naked eye underwater- so study attentively your subjects on marine life guidebooks before diving to learn what they real colors will look like once photographed. Notice also - once again - how the diagonal positioning of the main subject in relation to the general frame embellishes the final image, adding a ready-to-swoop-down quality to the small predator.

your mind. TTL allows you to concentrate on what you're doing or going to do, and avoid fidgeting with what you've just done. It will bring the fun back to underwater photography and will give you excellent results right from the start – there's no need to practice. TTL is practically perfect with macro photography and will work very well most of the times with wide-angle and fish-eye too – again, look at the pictures in this book and judge the results for yourself. And remember - if you don't like it or need more control you can always simply switch it off and go back to manual. I am so firmly convinced of the worth – nay, the need – for TTL that we've switched from analogue (i.e. film) to digital only very recently, when digital TTL finally became available after much

A dramatically lit portrait of the truly ugly and deadly venomous Stonefish *Synanceia horrida* echoes the terrifying sight of Peter Lorre in Karl Freund's *Mad Love* - lighting from below usually exaggerates and dramatizes strongly sculpted facial features.

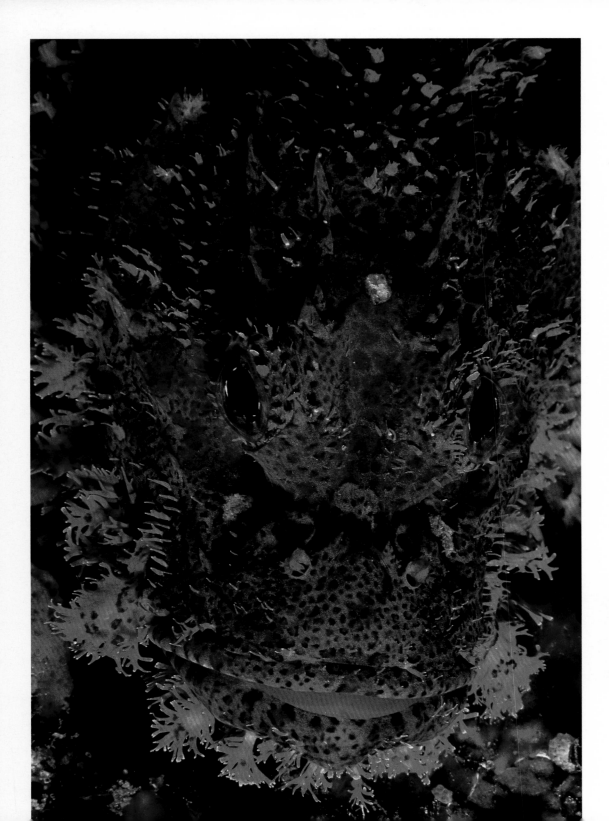

technical trial and tribulation. Why should we ignore the advantages offered by an innovative technology if they're so effective? Autofocus is much less discussed and taken almost for granted nowadays — almost everybody sticks to it, and when it has trouble working properly (in extremely low light situations, for example) you can always switch back to manual focusing. Wrist computers and modern BCDs aren't even discussed anymore, after all, being part and parcel of today's dive equipment — and yet they too were met with suspicion when first introduced. So my suggestion — a very personal one, as usual — is to adopt digital TTL as soon as possible and to place the possibility of using TTL protocols among your highest priorities when considering a camera system,

This demon-like portrait of a Tasselled scorpionfish *Scorpaenopsis oxycephala* was directly inspired by the atmospheric lighting utilized to dramatize Boris Karloff's gaunt, deathly pale make-up in James Whale's original *Frankenstein*.

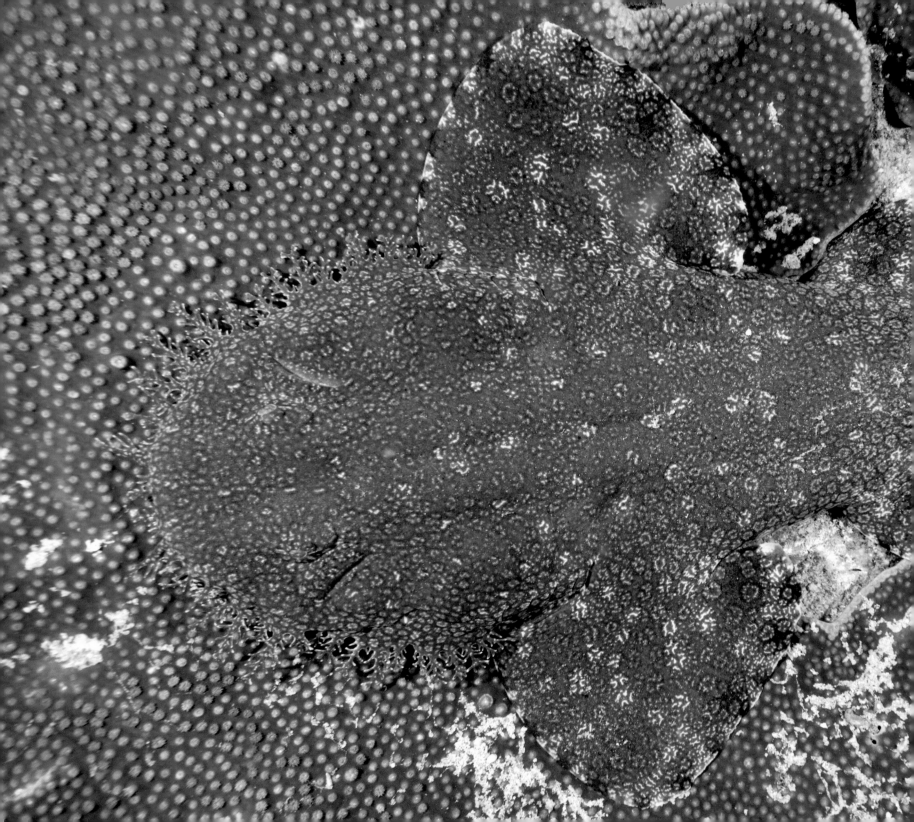

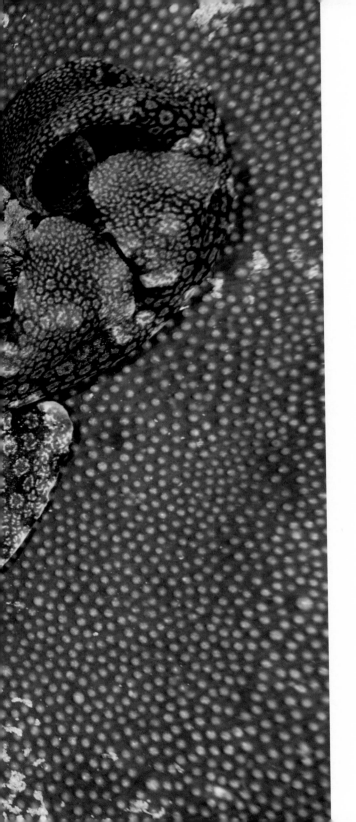

An apparently rather bland image reveals the extraordinary camouflage sported by Tasselled wobbegongs *Eucrossorhynus dasypogon*, bottom-dwelling carpet sharks which rely on disruptive patterns to literally disappear on the large flat coral colonies they commonly use as launching pads for their surprise attacks on passing fish. Note the bright white fake "eyes" and above all how the large rounded pectoral fins and the sharply contrasting, darker, usually curled tail conspire in mimicking the broad leaf-like convolutions of the coral colony to perfection. This is a good example of an apparently uninspired framing which is actually perfectly functional to the message the image wants to convey - in this case a cool and quite interesting scientific observation.

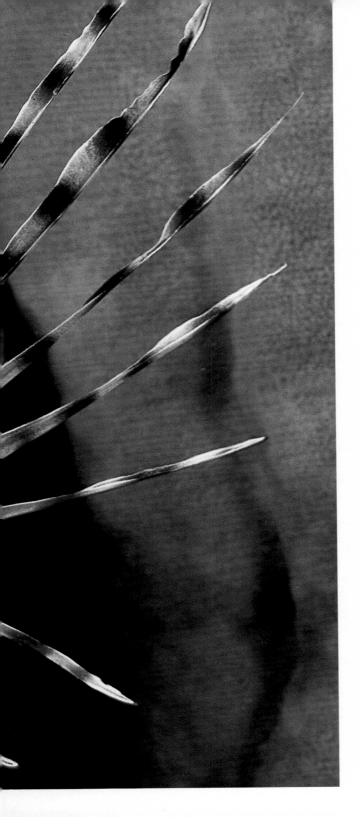

Photoshop or any similar software (there aren't many as good or flexible) will be invaluable in removing unwanted backscatter (which is not your fault as a photographer, at least most of the times) and maybe in slightly balancing the chromatic values of the photograph to your personal judgement and satisfaction if you're shooting in Raw. (If you're shooting Jpegs most of this will be done by your camera software anyway). But post-production cropping, sharpening, selective colour substitution, removal of undesired subjects and several other interesting digital tricks won't be able to save a bad picture. And even if they did – what's the point in doing it? You might as well digitally draw your image from scratch – it's not the photograph you have taken anymore. Why dive and take photographs at all – if afterwards you have to spend long, lonely hours in front of your laptop trying to salvage a bunch of lousy photos? No way! Make the best of what technology can offer you while you're underwater, concentrate on framing and lighting, learn to know and admire your subjects and above all enjoy what you're doing – it's all about sportsmanship, remember?

Another classic *Pterois volitans* Common lionfish portrait, redeemed in this instance by the graceful stance of the subject and by its unusual chromatic contrast with the bright purple sponge it is perched on. Never try prodding Lionfish or other scorpenids hoping to put them in a better position - they are ready to bolt and stick their highly venomous dorsal fin rays in the flesh of the disturber. The trick instead is to wait till the fish - alarmed by the enormous camera port and the looming strobes closing in like gigantic pincers - stands its ground and fans out is spectacular banner-like fins in a threatening display, hoping to scare the photographer away.

Chapter 4

SOARING IN THE BLUE
Why buoyancy control is so important for you

- Master your breathing techiques
- Be one with your subjects
- Respect the environment
- Check your bubbles

I have already expressed my somewhat harsh views on bad divers in the previous chapter, so I'll now try to humbly offer some advice on how to become a reasonably good one. If you're convinced you're a good diver already, well, feel free to skip this chapter – but maybe you'll miss some hopefully interesting opinions. Again, several of the concepts expressed in this chapter may sound excruciatingly obvious to experienced underwater photographers, and yet they should not be taken for granted.

First of all, being a good diver has little to do with actual physical strength (even if some muscles will come in handy in a ripping cur-

This wide-angle panoramic shot of a pristine coral reef at Layang Layang atoll in the South China Sea offers an excellent example of good buoyancy control, a technique which has to be fully mastered by any diver before even thinking of underwater photography. Buoyancy control minimizes damage to the environment, lowers fatigue levels and allows a close approach to most camera subjects.

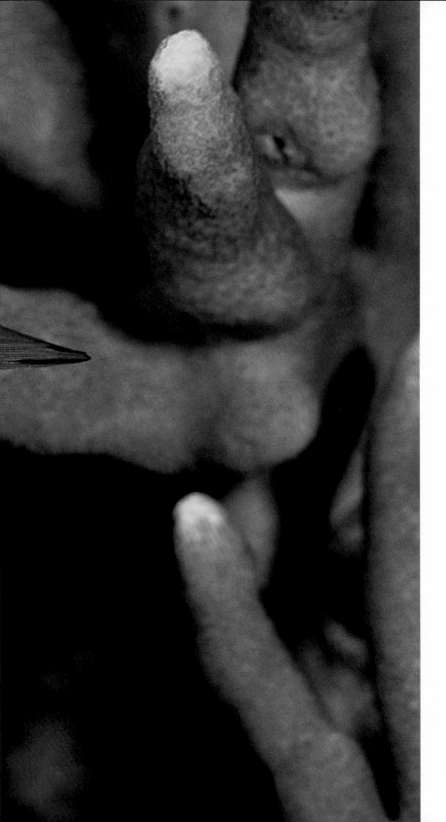

Gaudily colored Pyjama cardinalfish *Sphaeramia nematoptera* are exceptionally wary creatures, hiding during daytime among thick branching coral colonies, from which they gradually emerge at twilight to forage in the open. Shot using a Nikon 105mm at f.5.6 as a zoom with Fuji Velvia 50 film, this engaging portrait was taken in very clear water at Lankayan, Borneo, after almost ninety minutes of patient, slow stalking. Low air consumption is a must when trying to shoot shy, frustrating subjects such as this - even if digital technology has now made this type of tele-macro photography much more accessible.

rent), having much more to do with correct breathing techniques instead. Do you always inflate your BCD before/during a dive? Do you constantly deflate/adjust it during a dive? Do you carry a lot of extra weight on your belt or in your BCDs pockets in relation to your body mass and wetsuit thickness? Then you are a bad diver. Can you control your buoyancy by breathing alone? Can you hover in mid-water during your safety stop, remaining at a constant depth, by controlled breathing alone? Do you seldom or ever inflate/deflate your BCD during a dive, at least in normal conditions? Do you carry a minimal amount of weight in relation to your body mass and wetsuit thickness? Then you're a good diver, and chances are, becoming a good underwater photographer will be much easier for you. Let's examine in detail some of the opinions expressed above. One, body mass — i.e. the relationship between your height and your weight, related to sex and age. To offer an example, I'm 1.73 / 70 kgs and my wife Antonella is 1.73 / 60 kgs — we both are then reasonably well balanced in the scale, being quite trim but not underweight. In practice, being more or less fit — not overly muscled — will help you feeling more confident before and during a dive, will make the ordeal of kitting up less exhausting (especially under the blaze of a tropical sun) and will offer you better chances to feel at home underwater: you'll be more graceful and better organized. With an excellent respiration control, very little air consumption and a reasonably slim body we

A colorful wide-angle panorama shot on a Maldivian reef with a Nikon 20mm at f.8 using Fuji Velvia 50 film. A common mistake committed by beginners is shooting reefs from above, usually resulting in flat, colorless images. Shooting from a low point and keeping at least part of the water surface in the frame usually results instead in interesting, attention-getting patterns, especially if some wave action is present. Good buoyancy control is of paramount importance when shooting in a current along reef walls and slopes.

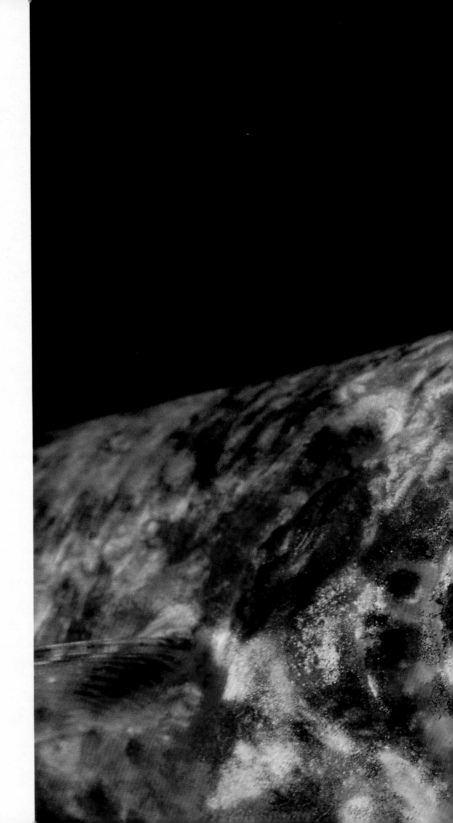

Lizardfish *Synodus* spp. are benthic, static predators capable however of unexpected, very fast dashes when hunting or disturbed - getting close enough to shoot a portrait like this one (Nikon 105mm, f.22, Fuji Velvia 50 film) requests a very slow, indirect approach and lots of patience. Again, low air consumption and good buoyancy control are extremely important when stalking wary, shy subjects and not shooting on the spur of the moment.

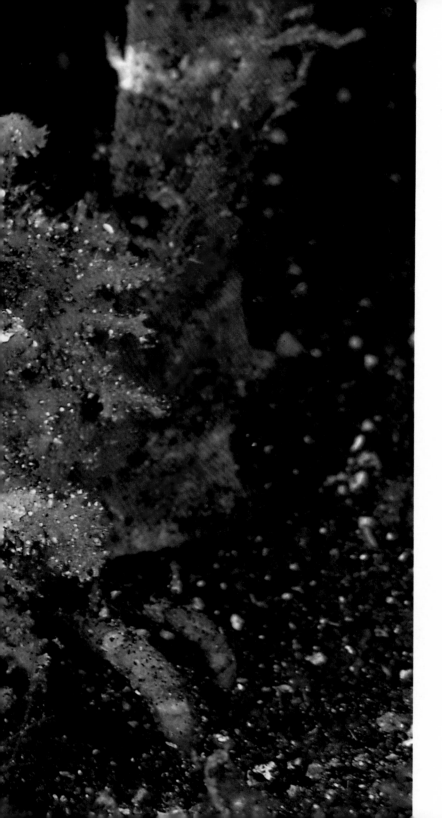

Underwater photographers don't want to end up with an elbow or a
knee carelessly hitting the dorsal fin rays of the aptly named Devil
scorpionfish *Inimicus didactylus*, whose grotesque, menacing looks are on
a par with the potent venom it can inject if trod upon. "Muck diving" - ie
searching for strange, rare subjects on silty, muddy bottoms, often in bad
visibility - requires the utmost care as most subjects are often hidden in
the sand, often being highly venomous and ready to impale clumsy divers
kneeling on the substrate.

Guest
Photographer

Eric
CHENG

USA

Canon D60
Canon 16-35mm
Sea & Sea Housing
Ikelite DS125 dual strobes

Shooting on the surface is usually exceedingly difficult, as the human body naturally tends to float at shallow depth - especially when a highly buoyant wetsuit is worn. Undaunted by the difficulties presented by the situation, Eric Cheng shows here what can be achieved with this brilliant, dynamic portrait of a Juvenile Loggerhead turtle *Caretta caretta* being released into the wild at Palm Beach, Florida.

can do without extra useless weight (as another example, I normally wear 4 kgs and Antonella wears 3 kgs – needed almost exclusively to help stabilizing when doing finely-tuned macro photography). Unnecessary extra weight or an excess of weight needed by an overweight person is always the cause of unbalanced postures, extra fatigue and occasional downright danger. Being over or even underweight, on the contrary, will tire you sooner (like in most other physical activities) and will occasionally make you more dependent on others, lowering your self-confidence and affecting your ability to concentrate underwater. A trim body – supported by a positive mental attitude, as usual - will also be very useful in achieving a correct way

A more sedate and relaxed chelonian - a mature Green turtle *Chelonia mydas* - rests on the sand by the reef at Sipadan, in Malaysian Borneo. Notice how this image - shot with a Nikon 20mm at f.16 - makes good use of the graceful model in the background to balance the main subject in the foreground.

of breathing underwater, possibly the most important factor in feeling at home in such a potentially hostile environment.

Breathing correctly in this context means breathing little – if you're coming out of the water after 50 minutes of normal diving in 27° C water with less than 80 bar showing on your pressure gauge, it means you're breathing too much, needlessly fatiguing your body and generally betraying nervousness and a lack of confidence. How can you expect to take good pictures if you keep on worrying about your air? And why should you be gulping all that air down, anyway? If you're gasping for air it can only mean you're scared and not enjoying yourself – so relax and control yourself. Practice on your breathing rhythms while on land, adopt yoga-like simple concentration techniques and put them in practice during your next dive – you'll soon learn and will achieve surprising results. Diving can occasionally be a demanding activity, but it doesn't necessarily need to be a strenuous one. After all, when you're peacefully strolling in town you do not breathe that hard, and it's quite surprising how far one can move underwater with little effort, if feeling at ease. There's no need to keep on finning madly like you were running amok on a speeding bicycle – fish don't do that! Adopt slow, stiff-legged strokes for power or relaxed, occasional frog-leaps to conserve strength. So this brings us to another matter – conserving energy to get longer, more fruit-

Incredibly beautiful, very fast and extremely active, Peacock mantis shrimp *Odontodactylus scyllarus* are occasionally observed hurriedly scooting among the coral rubble at shallow depth on the reefs of the Indo-Pacific. Being able to properly photograph one requires a high degree of control in buoyancy and the slimmest of equipment to avoid damaging the corals or getting snagged in their glassy, sharp ramifications.

ful dives, and to be able to use that extra kick when needed. You might find yourself in an emergency where you'll suddenly and unexpectedly need to use all your remaining strength and air – I still remember a frightful downcurrent which pulled me and my exhaled bubbles deep, deep down for a few terrifying minutes while photographing sunfish in the ice-cold waters off Bali – and even if such occurrences might be rare, they do happen, and being physically and psychologically prepared for them can mean the difference between being scared and being dead. So teach yourself to quietly relax, to control your emotions, to regulate your breathing and, most importantly, not to stretch your limits. If the prospect of a certain dive scares you, don't do it! This is

Periclemenes brevicarpalis Commensal shrimp are often observed on large anemones, offering a beautiful, contrasting background to their colorful and partially transparent armoured body. Getting close enough - this shot was taken with a Nikon 105mm at f.22 - requires care, patience and a good trim.

supposed to be fun and you're supposed to enjoy doing it, so don't feel guilty if you turn away from something which worries you — you wouldn't enjoy it and you might even put yourself in danger. Think it over and do it when you'll feel more confident — dive somewhere else in the meantime, there's always something beautiful to see and photograph underwater.

Which brings us to the art of seeing, a quite obviously important aspect for good photography. Generally speaking, in most famous dive localities around the globe, big groups of divers are led around like mindless cattle, frantically running from point A to point B — and if one dares to stop for a second, he or she will often get

Veined octopus *Amphioctopus marginatus* are usually very small, occasionally numerous and invariably found on silty, mucky bottoms. Clumsy divers - if not careful - will rapidly kick up large quantities of silt on such substrates, reducing visibility and making photography problematic or impossible.

immediately rebuked by an impatient guide, or even by a petulant fellow diver. Divers are managed, not guided around and shown about.
That won't do at all! If you want to take good pictures you must be
able to move on your own, alone if very experienced or at least
accompanied by your trusted and well-tried dive buddy, calmly looking around for subjects and generally enjoying your dive – think of
this as a gentle, pleasant, slow stroll while looking at beautiful paintings in a museum, not as a neurotic competition to see who gets out
of the water first. You're diving to admire wonderful things, not to just
to demonstrate swimming prowess – if you simply want to swim then
go to a swimming pool. Sounds stupid? Of course it does, but take a
look at a guided group of divers anywhere and see for yourself. So –
be relaxed, be confident, breath as little and regularly as possible and,
above all, try to dive in a buddy pair or at least in a motivated small
group which may be patient enough to understand your needs (most
divers can't stand diving together with photographers and cannot
accept the idea of one spending his or her full dive in an area the size
of a small room – it seems we're very boring company). Taking your
time will offer you unexpected opportunities to see much, much
more than the others will, and your chances as a photographer will
dramatically increase.

Ornate ghostpipefish *Solenostomus paradoxus* are usually quite mobile: this portrait of a
colorful pair- with the larger female brooding a clutch of eggs in the ventral pouch
formed by her specialized pelvic fins - was taken with a Nikon 105mm at f.22 and
required a prolonged hovering with the shallowest of breathings.
At such small framing and focusing distances - when depth of field is truly minimal -
every inhalation or slight change in buoyancy due to the expansion of lungs can easily
throw the subject out of focus.

Correct, ingrained breathing techniques borne out of self-confidence and serenity will naturally bring to easy, instinctive buoyancy control. Can you hover face-down with your nose a few inches above the muck, comfortably holding your cumbersome camera rig, your immobile fins pointing well away from the bottom – by controlled, shallow, slow breathing alone? This is what we mean by good buoyancy control – and you're going to need it if you are interested in taking good macro shots without harassing your tiny subjects (which obviously should go without saying) or, even worse, damaging the delicate environment they live in. Above all, always remember you're a privileged witness and, somehow, perhaps even a self-appointed custodian of what you see and admire down there, so don't be clumsy or careless – practice your buoyancy skills to perfection to avoid crashing on the bottom or among the corals like a deflated balloon when trying to take a photo. Once you have learnt how to do it, you'll be amazed by how much a little more or a little less air in your lungs can accomplish. Complete buoyancy and breathing control will also allow you to closely approach very small and shy camera subjects such as bottom-dwelling shrimp gobies – remember that the perception of sound waves and vibrations by marine animals is very different from ours, and what sounds like the faint hissing of a working regulator to us probably sounds like a terrifying wail of hellish noise to them, so it's always better to minimize intrusion. In some cases you'll need to

Uncluttered kit, no dangling hoses and perfect buoyancy control are required to enter the thick bushes of Black coral growing on steep walls and drop-offs which are the exclusive home of the fascinating Saw-blade shrimp *Tozeuma armatum*, a master of camouflage shorter than a little finger. Notice once more how the subject has been framed diagonally, choosing to shoot at f.16 rather than at f.22 to reduce depth of field to have it stand out from the background. Focusing correctly on such small subjects while free-floating in front of a wall requests the utmost concentration.

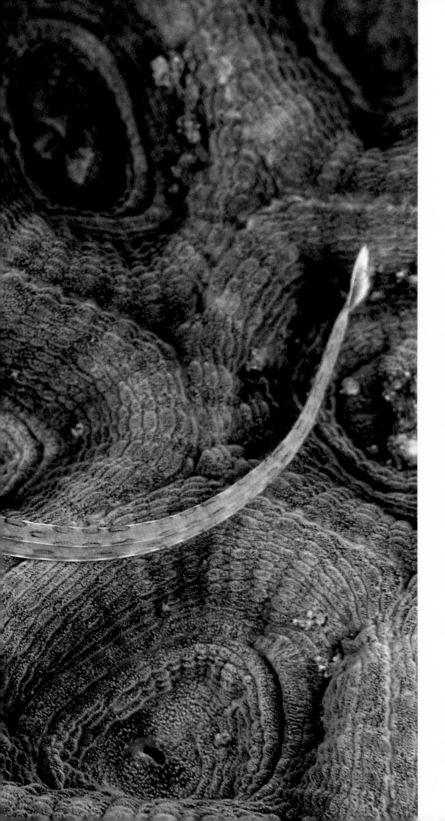

Beautifully framed on a sculptured, textured landscape of coral polyp cups, this Orange-spotted pipefish *Corythoichthys ocellatus* was spotted while muck-diving in the Lembeh Strait - quite an unexpected but very welcome find. The elongated shape of the pipefish contrasts pleasantly with the rounded, fat shapes of the coral mound it is crawling on, creating an interesting, attractive contrast. Relaxed, unhurried dives will often produce satisfying results for the discriminating underwater photographer- especially when doing macro.

lie still on the sand bottom for several long minutes on end, waiting for your subjects to peek out of their burrow again — and then you'll be glad you've learnt to economize and correctly administer your air reserves. And since we're on the subject, let me add my own coal to the fires of controversy — we do not agree at all with the "no-gloves" policy adopted by several dive resorts and marine reserve authorities worldwide. Not being allowed to occasionally touch the substrate — preferably on dead-coral spots and exercising selective finger-tip control, quite easily accomplished underwater by proficient divers — will commonly and regularly result in immensely greater damage to the reef inflicted by clumsy, troubled divers trying to position

Perfect buoyancy control is very important for the photographer, but it is an absolute must for the model. Notice how the elegant, graceful body attitude of Antonella, hovering in the background, complements to perfection this small school of Striped bigeye bream *Gnathodentex aureolineatus* photographed with a fish-eye at Sipadan in Malaysian Borneo.

themselves by kicking their fins alone, which as we all know are a lot tougher and stiffer than a gloved finger. Enforcing a "no-gloves" policy to the average inexperienced diver, generally unable to finely-tune his or her buoyancy skills, is tantamount to inviting rapid disaster on untouched reefs. So much for good intentions! On a different note, controlling buoyancy to a fine degree by mastering breathing techniques will also allow you to become a stable camera platform in open water, giving you better chances of getting satisfying results with pelagic subjects – it's quite easy to damage an eardrum if you keep on changing depth without realizing it while concentrating on an incoming whale shark and are too busy to equalize. Controlled and graceful

Getting this fish-eye shot of a diving Yellow-lipped sea krait *Laticauda colubrina* required more than thirty minutes of patient stalking. Finally the sea snake rose to the surface, gulped down some fresh air and then speedily undulated towards the bottom - and the camera dome in which it saw itself reflected. One has to stop breathing to avoid getting any bubbles in the shot.

A young male Spine-cheek anemonefish *Premnas biaculeatus* emerges -
one could almost say merrily - from its colorful host. Freezing the action
at exactly the most desirable time is what we should aim for in this case
- notice how the eyes and the fins are perfectly balanced in this image.
There is no use in frantically shooting one picture after the other in these
cases - take your time, carefully observe patterns of behavior, then relax
and click by reflex, letting your instinct take charge.

Roger
HORROCKS
South Africa

Nikon D100
Nikon 10.5mm fish-eye
Sea & Sea housing
ambient light

Another exceptionally atmospheric image by Roger Horrocks, a perfectly balanced, dark underwater ballet in which the huge tiger shark *Galeocerdo cuvier* female in the foreground, the free-diving underwater photographer in the middle and the second circling tiger shark in the far background all play their role to perfection, as they had been rehearsing it for ages past. With its players suspended in an unnerving no-man's-land between light and darkness, a foggy limbo between the clarity of the surface above and the gloom of the yawning deep below, this is evocative, operatic underwater camerawork at its best - a no-frills exercise of the mind more than a show of modern digital technology and a moving testament to the grace and power of the great sharks of the abyss.

A sharp, dynamic portrait of a large Oceanic whitetip shark *Carcharhinus longimanus* sweeping in for a close check from the bright blue sea encircling the Brothers Islands in the Southern Red Sea. Taken with a 20mm at f.8 on Fuji Provia 100, this much-published image makes good use of the incoming Rainbow runners in the background and the purposeful, muscular curving motion of its main subject. Large pelagic sharks can be quite inquisitive, often approaching divers very closely - one has to be very alert to body language in these occasions as such encounters can rapidly turn very dangerous. In this occasion the whole encounter lasted forty-five minutes, and ended when we were forced to exit the water by the arrival of two more Oceanic whitetips.

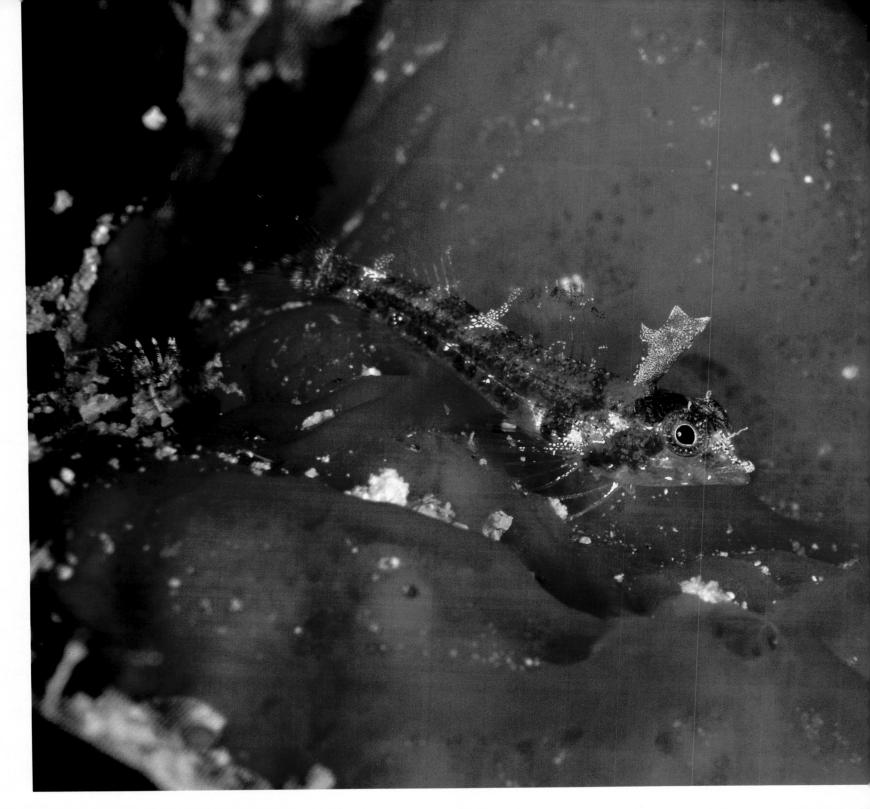

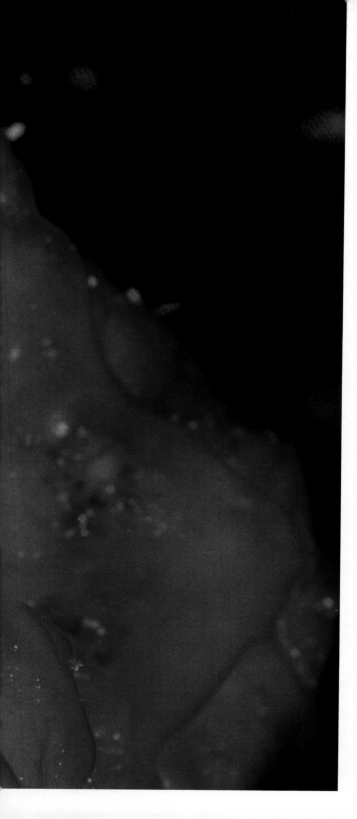

body movements, in turn, will allow you to get closer to your subjects, while slow, relaxed, shallow exhaling will be less annoying to most fish species (this is why professional photographers and film-makers use bubble-free rebreathers to approach skittish subjects, such as scalloped hammerheads). Breathing control will also come in handy when attempting that masterful trick – shooting upwards with the camera lens pointing towards the surface: there's nothing more troublesome than an uncontrolled stream of noisy bubbles bursting away from your regulator at the wrong moment and invading your field of view to spoil an otherwise beautiful, perfectly-framed image.

A tiny Crowned triplefin *Enneapterygius pusillus* regally sits on its bright red perch - all two centimeters of it. Perfectly camouflaged, it was only detected by the rapid flicking of its first dorsal fin, used to signal to rival males in territorial disputes. A relaxed, at ease attitude while diving will always allow underwater photographers to notice much more than they would hurrying along in search of the next subject. Taken with a Nikon 105mm at f.22 on Fuji Velvia 50, this image was shot on a vertical wall at 40 meters of depth while diving at Barracuda Point on Sipadan, in Malaysian Borneo.

TARGETS OF OPPORTUNITY
Tally Ho! Bandits at Twelve O'Clock High!

- Patrolling the big blue
- The "killer" instinct
- Always on the lookout
- Working on routines
- Dealing with large animals
- Do's and Don'ts

Since I was a child, I've always been a sucker for WWII-era air combat movies – you know, flying goggles, white scarves, worn-out leather flying jackets, "*Look out, Red One – you've got a bandit on your tail!*" and all that heroic and slightly disenchanted stuff. Elegantly soaring in the blue sky above, skimming down at tree-top height or duelling among towering bright clouds, fighter planes of old war movies have always reminded me, somehow, of scuba diving. Come to think of it, similarities abound. Just like fighter and bomber crews, we divers do kit up in messy barracks and in jolly confusion, attend pre-mission (or rather pre-dive) briefings in front of a chalkboard and in religious silence (with

A portrait of a big Oceanic whitetip shark *Carcharhinus longimanus* coming in from the blue in the Red Sea, taken with a 20mm at f.8 at 15 meters in open water. When photographing large, unpredictable and sometimes potentially dangerous pelagic predators in the open sea it is exceedingly important be able to freely concentrate on the subjects and their body language - camera settings, buoyancy control, air consumption, depth and duration of dive must be checked continuously and automatically, without being distracted by mere technical details. Care was taken to have none of the pilotfish *Naucrates ductor* in the shot interfere with the majestic, streamlined beauty of the main subject.

Guest
Photographer

Fiona
AYERST
South Africa

Nikon D200
Nikon 20mm
Sea & Sea housing
Sea & Sea YS120 dual strobes

Bull - also known as Zambezi - sharks *Carcharhinus leucas* are big, bulky, brutish coastal predators with an unsavoury reputation and the capability to swim up rivers for hundreds of chilometers. Fiona Ayerst gets the perfect shot of one of these rarely observed hunters off the current-swept coast of Mozambique at Ponta Mamoli, shooting at exactly the right moment to catch the rippling skin on the muscular, supple back of the shark and its small, yellowish, staring eyes focusing coldly into her lens. In the lower right corner of the original image another photographer is partially visible - the plain admission of having removed it in Photoshop with the cloning tool does not detract in the least from the raw, wild power emanating like a primeval glow from the oncoming shark.

GUEST PHOTOGRAPHER

the occasional fellow diver showing signs of half-concealed anxiety, just like the newcomer to the squadron), swap silly jokes and oft-repeated stupid anecdotes in good camaraderie, and we are also taken to our starting or take-off spots in a group (pilots by the airport jeep, divers by their boat) to finally find ourselves all alone, silently suspended in a dark blue world. Our survival – as it happened with old-time aircrews – depends on the correct usage and proper working of a rather basic mechanical apparatus, and if WWII pilots would readily don their oxygen masks at altitude, we have to rely on a regular, dependable supply of compressed air instead. Like fighter plane pilots, we usually are fiercely independent, and yet at the same time curiously dependent on our wingman – sorry, I mean our dive buddy. And of course the debriefing after the mission – usually spent with a few beers back at the resort or on the pier - sees us talking and laughing loud, making exaggerated, swooping gestures with our hands and proudly swapping stories about "how good that was". Are you starting to see the similarities?

If you do, and have stopped laughing by now, you'll understand why we commonly adopt the "fighter pilot" set of mind when patrolling the big blue world, be it the open ocean or the deep sea facing a steep wall. Well, at least I do! It's fun, and it works – you'll often see stuff other divers miss because they're too busy waiting for their dive guide to

A portrait of two patrolling Grey reef sharks *Carcharhinus amblyrhynchos* swimming with elegant determination and in line astern towards the waiting camera lens. The surrounding barren reef scenery and the angle of approach of the subjects add a sense of urgency to the scene - this animals mean business! Shooting from a distance often allows the photographer to portray his subjects in their own environment, adding another dimension to the image, but being able to add a personal creative touch to a strictly behavioral (mating, feeding) image is often extremely difficult - and probably not even necessary in most cases.

Guest
Photographer

Doug
PERRINE
USA

Nikonos RS
Nikonos RS 13mm fish-eye
ambient light

Beautiful but bulky, the Nikonos RS was widely publicized as a techno-logical breakthrough at the time of its launch, but was not loved by most and often abandoned soon after, bringing a premature end to its production. In the hands of a master it could - and still can - provide sterling service, however, as any other basically sound camera system. Doug Perrine uses it to freeze this whirling bloody dance of death as a spiralling school of silhouetted spinner dolphins scythes dramatically through a gigantic, shimmering baitball. Such fast action - often taking place for just a few frenzied seconds - forces the photographer to dive (or even free-dive) without heavy, cumbersome strobes, only relying on available ambient light. Notice the faultless composition of the shot, in which every single element falls naturally in place without interfering with the others.

Guest
Photographer

Tony WU

Japan

Canon 1D MkII
Canon 15mm fish-eye
Subal housing
ambient light

Striking a perfect balance between mass and elegance, Tony Wu succeeds in avoiding any unsightly fish-eye corner distortion in this beautiful blue-water portrait of two graceful Humpbacks whales *Megaptera novaeangliae* off the coast of Tonga. The diagonal, curved posture of the big mother beneath is gently counterpointed by the straight horizontal line presented by her smaller calf above - one complementing the other and adding to the feeling of maternal bonding powerfully transmitted by this peaceful underwater ballet in slow-motion. It takes great empathy with the subject and a lot of physical stamina to shoot such beautifully balanced images while free-diving in the open ocean.

show them something. First, whenever we dive along a steep wall facing the open ocean, we adopt a "fighter patrol" position in relation to each other – the leader in the front and at a lower "altitude", the wingman (yes, the buddy!) several meters behind and above. Distances vary, but this formation allows us great flexibility, and in this way the leader is free to bolt into the blue or dive down fast in case something interesting (and usually fleeting) should show up, knowing that the faithful wingman/buddy is always covering his/her back, letting him concentrating on the photography and ready to bring him back to reality in case anything goes wrong. Getting too involved in the action might result in the flight leader/main photographer to go too deep without realizing it, or lose sight of the wall, or get caught into a tricky and dangerous current. Risks abound in such quick-decision situations, and it's good knowing that you've got a guardian angel looking after your back. Especially when – exactly as in the case of WWII fighter pilots – the so-called "killer instinct" or "target fixation" takes the photographer over – enthusiastically tailing a big shoal of hammerheads rapidly disappearing in the blue only to find himself lost, alone, too deep, with not enough air left and too much decompression to do. Such things should never happen obviously, and yet do so all the time, occasionally with serious results – so always have a trusty wingman covering your back! Having your dive buddy behind you and at shallower depth will also constantly provide you with a readily positioned model for upwards-

Technically imperfect and shot from too far away to be a good photo, this image of a rarely sighted Pelagic thresher shark *Alopias pelagicus* is nonetheless included to demonstrate what fast reflexes and finely tuned routines can achieve. For several years the only decent image available anywhere of this beautiful species, it offered me less than five seconds to decide to shoot in available light, switch off the strobes, change aperture to a suitable f-stop, focus and click - five seconds only, and then the shark was back to the depths it had come from. Due to the rarity of its subject, this image was subsequently published a great number of times all over the world despite its mediocre quality.

Chapter 5 • TARGETS OF OPPORTUNITY

195

The gigantic Napoleon wrasse *Chelinus undulatus* has sadly become a very rare sight everywhere since its flesh - and especially its thick lips - fetch exceptionally high prices in Chinese markets and restaurants, particularly in Hong Kong. A 20mm used to be the lens of choice to portray at its colorful best this peaceful, door-sized reef dweller - a lens wide enough to take it all in when close, sharp enough at the same time to do full justice to its exquisite, intricate green and blue markings. Despite the efforts by a very few dedicated individuals, large individuals of most marine species - including sharks, sailfish, marlin and swordfish - have become almost impossible to see underwater - a sad sign of the times and a frightening omen for the future.

A female Grey reef shark *Carcharhinus amblyrhynchos* passes overhead at
Maya Thilla in the Maldives. When diving in groups to view and hopefully
photograph resident sharks or mantas at a given location - as it often
happens in the Maldives - the other divers are often a distracting
presence, both for the photographer underwater and in the resulting
images. Great care must be taken to avoid spoiling an otherwise
perfect shot - even if it is often possible to remove
unwanted presences later on in Photoshop.

aimed panoramic shots, hopefully with a big fish and a nice sunburst somewhere in your frame, should the opportunity arise. Diving in well-disciplined, organized pairs — or, occasionally, even in threes, especially if you've been lucky enough to have the local dive guide all to your-selves — will greatly increase the chances of a good sighting if you also adopt another trick developed by old-time fighter pilots, i.e. the con-stant swivelling of your head around, looking continuously at all quad-rants of the open sea in the hope of catching that distant revealing glint of an approaching big fish. Again, this might sound quite obvious, and yet a great percentage of underwater photographers and scuba divers generally doggedly follow on in a single file, stubbornly looking down at the bare bottom slowly rolling under their bellies, without ever tak-ing the trouble of craning their neck in some other direction — miss-ing unbelievable photographic opportunities and precious encounters. In one occasion we've witnessed a big school of scalloped hammer-heads coming in from the open ocean and literally pass by a line of very conscientious, inexperienced divers swimming by a vertical wall, who all kept looking religiously down without realizing that scores of two-meter long sharks were gleefully eyeing them from just a few meters away! On the contrary, we've been able to identify approaching Oceanic whitetip sharks in the open sea from a long, long way off, being able to set our camera and get ready for the chance of a good shot — only by sighting what we first identified as a small shoal of closely-

The best of only three shots which were fleetingly allowed us when a small school of Devil rays *Mobula tarapacana* swam by the shallow coral reef at Layang Layang in the South China Sea. Having literally no time to reach for the strobes and switch them off - to shoot, as I would have preferred, in available light - I clicked off right away with a 20mm at f.5.6, hoping the exceptional visibility of the dive site would result in no backscatter. Luckily, the water was perfectly clear and the strobes' flash actually slightly highlighted the immaculate ventral surfaces of the overflying squadron without spoiling the image.

Stephen
WONG

Hong Kong

Nikonos RS
Nikonos RS 13mm fish-eye
ambient light

Once more, a great photographer gets spectacular results from a much-maligned camera system - Stephen Wong portrays a small pod of rarely sighted Dusky dolphins playing on the surface while diving off the coast of Patagonia in Argentina. Used - as it should whenever possible - at literally touching distance from the subjects, his 13mm fish-eye distorts the corners of the image and the surface horizon, at the same time however allowing precious details to emerge from the surrounding frigid gloom - notice how the dolphin in the background is actually swimming belly-up and how beautifully the reflections from the surface light up the animals' otherwise dark backs.

packed light-coloured fish in the distance, and which after a few seconds revealed itself to be the bright white fin tips of these large and beautiful pelagic predators instead. So we have taught ourselves a lesson – if fighter pilots used to say they needed to have one extra set of eyes in the back of their necks to survive every mission, we need to keep on swivelling our head around – looking up, down, right, left, even behind us. Do not stop ever from looking around, always remember that big marine animals may come unexpectedly and from all directions – and if you or your wingman sight a target, do not use your radio! No blow horns, no noisy underwater gadgets – even a small shaker might scare your big subject way, so whenever possible resort to sign language to alert your buddy of that big beautiful fish coming your way.

I've mentioned the fighter pilot's "killer instinct" above. If we strip the expression of all its horrifying connotations of man-against-man violence, as we obviously should in all this just-for-fun comparison with air combat, we're left with an automatic, instinctive reaction which experienced photographers know well – the action triggered by pure reflex. Zen and the Art of Underwater Photography, I told you! Hands move swiftly, gears are adjusted without even looking, strobes are turned off automatically if we want to shoot in ambient light (as we generally should with very large or far-off subjects such as whale sharks, big cetaceans or dolphin pods), stiff-legged power-finning kicks

Dynamic action suddenly explodes on a shallow sunlit reef as a squadron of marauding Bluefin trevallies *Caranx melampygus* scythes at full speed through the ranks of an enormous school of panicking Fusiliers. Realizing almost immediately such repeated, violent attacks always came from the same direction, I positioned myself accordingly behind a coral bommie, succeeding to get this dynamic shot on the next occasion - notice how the use of perspective adds depth to the scene. Close observation of behavioral patterns is of paramount importance if one is striving to obtain good photographic results in such occasions - together with the use of strobes and high shutter speeds to freeze the speeding predators and their fleeing, frantically maneuvering preys.

Quickly switching the strobes off and automatically adjusting the aperture resulted in this graceful study of a Leopard (or Zebra) *Stegostoma fasciatum* shark passing by in the rapidly fading light of sunset on one of Lankayan's shallow reefs, on the coast of Borneo. Being able to correctly decide - in a handful of seconds - when available ambient light might offer a better result than artificial flash illumination can make the difference between a reasonably good image and a very bad one.

Guest
Photographer

John
SCARLETT

USA

Nikon D2X
Nikon 12-24mm
Subal ND2 housing
Inon Z220 dual strobes

Horizontally cropped for publication, this superb and highly unusual image shot by John Scarlett at Isla Guadalupe in Mexico speaks volumes about the immense power and the gracefulness shown underwater by Great white sharks *Carcharodon carcharias*.

Here a male (in the foreground, identified by the large claspers) and a female - very rarely sighted together, let alone photographed - calmly and confidently glide by in an exquisitely framed shot, the dappled light from the sunlit surface playing on their dark smooth backs. Diving with such powerful and intimidating predators - often in difficult sea conditions - requests calm, self-assuredness and the right mental attitude from the photographer. This image is a testimony to the flexibility offered underwater by the new zooms (John used the Nikon 12-24mm) - difficult to master, these are lenses which should whenever possible be employed underwater at their widest focal length as close-up wide-angles (and not, as many beginners do, as telephotos to get close to distant subjects). Always remember that the more water there is between your lens and the subject, the less sharp and colorful your final image will be!

in like a high-altitude engine power-booster. Open-water encounters with large pelagic animals are rare and above all usually fleeting – such free ranging creatures rarely pause to pose for us, and often swim gracefully as speedily, as anybody who has been lucky enough to dive or snorkel with a whale shark can testify. This is where one more habit developed by old-time fighter pilots might come in handy – the practicing of routines. Whenever a WWII-era flyer found himself engaged in combat, he'd immediately have to transform himself in a multi-handed piano virtuoso – frantically adjusting trim and gas mixture with his left hand, holding and moving the control stick with his right one and pressing the gun lever with his right thumb, jockeying controls with his feet, re-cock-

A good example of the constant need to crane your neck in all directions while diving deep. Recognizing the good opportunity, this atmospheric image of a backlit Whitetip reef shark *Triaenodon obesus* with a flash-lit, large and very colorful soft coral colony in the foreground was shot at 40 meters with a 16mm fish-eye set at f.8 at South Point in Sipadan, Malaysian Borneo.

ing jammed guns if needed, constantly checking gauges of all sorts on his dashboard, from the altitude indicator to the ammo counters, and all the while desperately trying to survive while streaking — occasionally upside-down - at 800 km/h in the sky. Now, underwater photographers will hopefully seldom find themselves in such a dangerous predicament, but sooner or later you'll find yourself stalking (not chasing — a good underwater photographer will never chase his subjects) some big fish in open water, possibly in a strong current and far away from land or boat. Facing an oncoming whale shark - with only a few seconds available to act in the hope of getting a good shot - or finding oneself among zooming, hunting sailfish attacking a baitball in the middle of the ocean

A slightly more carefully composed image, shot with the same lens and at the same location, shows how useful it can be having your buddy swimming above, always keeping an eye on you and ready to react to your hand signals. The large gorgonian with the floating, curving school of basslets in front of it proved an irresistible temptation - and Antonella was quick to position herself correctly above.

Guest
Photographer

Fiona
AYERST
South Africa

Nikon F100
Nikon 16mm fish-eye
Sea & Sea housing
Sea & Sea YS120 dual strobes

Manta pictures abound, but it takes an artist's eye for color and composition to create a novel, arresting image of these beautiful, graceful
subjects. Fiona Ayerst recognizes the wonderful opportunity and
reacts accordingly, shooting at exactly the right time to create a colorful tapestry with a school of blood-red Crescent tail bigeyes
Priacanthus hamrur in the foreground and a huge, suspended Manta
Manta birostris ghostly floating in the gloomy background, perfectly
poised against the sunburst. Underwater magic - evoked by freezing
time and movement when the photographer's inner creativity instinctively recognizes the opportunities offered by chance.

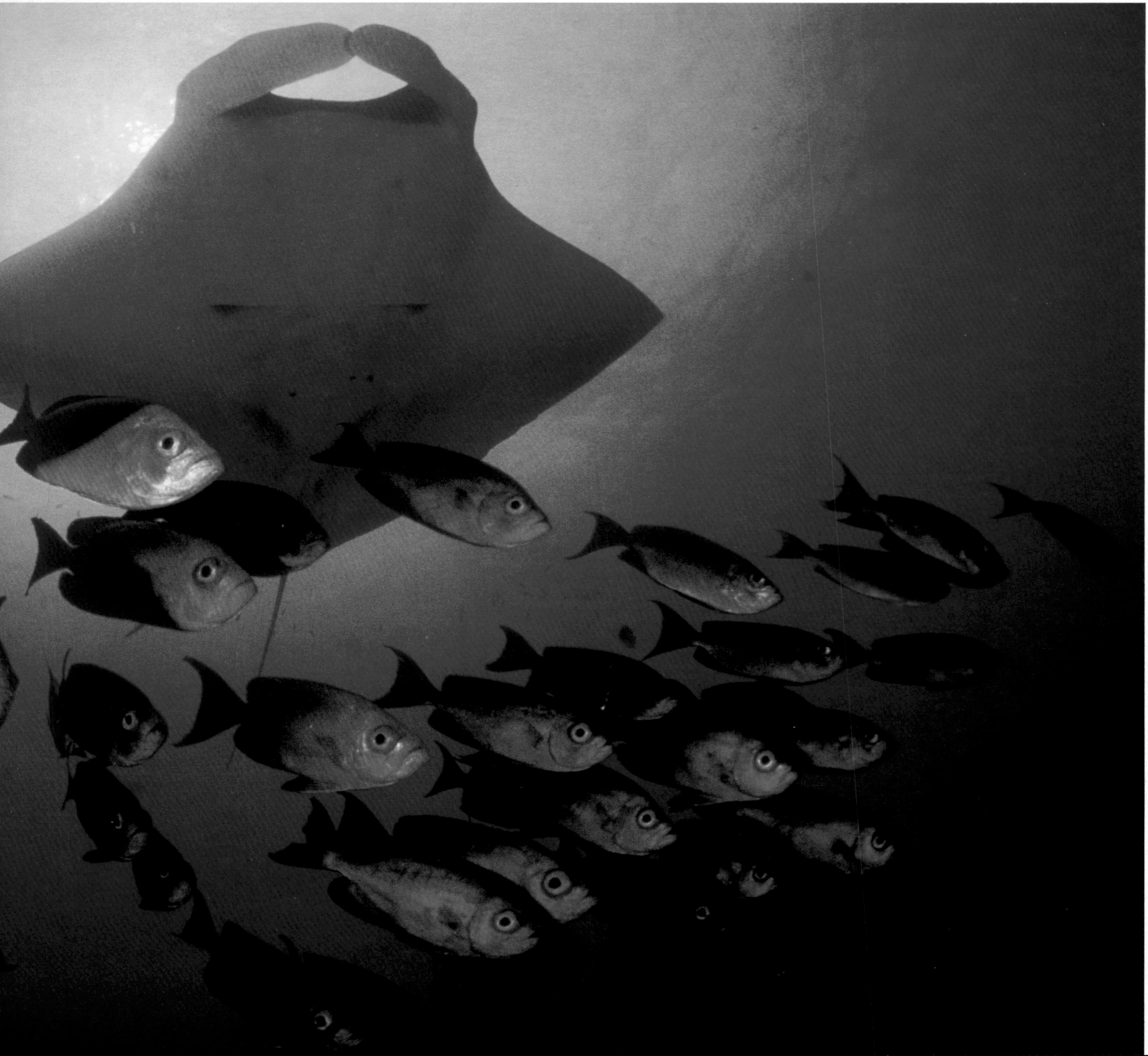

will get the adrenaline rushing, further complicating matters. Concentrating on your picture is what you want, but doing so will expose you to the possibility of committing mistakes – from misjudging your actual depth to missing the shot of a lifetime because you're simply too excited and frantically fumbling around. As our by-now old friend the fighter pilot cited above, you'll then have to teach yourself routines, until you'll be going through the basics without even realizing it. Such routines are nothing to worry about, and in fact simply consist in constantly checking the depth you're at and your remaining no-deco time by looking at your dive computer, continuously monitoring your air supply (these are the basics obviously, and yet lots of beginners forget to do so), and at the same time regularly controlling your camera settings and the on/off switches of your strobes. Always remember that your camera housing's external controls are seldom lockable (nor they should be), and as such they can be very easily switched around without realizing it while still on the boat or during the actual diving – never take anything for granted ("*But I was absolutely sure I had started my dive with my camera aperture correctly set at f.8, how can it be all my shots are grossly overexposed at f2.8 now?*" – Because you inadvertently moved your aperture gear, dummy. "*Oh my god, I'm lost, my autofocus gear is broken*" – no it's not, you just disengaged it – just take a look at that little knob on your housing's side) and always re-check - if at all possible - before composing your final shot. Strobes can be tricky too

Admittedly less inspired and not as colorful as the previous image, this shot of a truly gigantic Marbled stingray *Taeniura melanospilos* was taken with a 20mm wide-angle at f.8 and twin strobes when the animal suddenly passed overhead, floating and flapping in slow-motion like a nightmarish magic carpet, in the dark foggy waters of Cocos Island, off the Pacific Ocean coast of Costa Rica. At the very least, this is a rather unusual image which offers a novel and welcome perspective on a much-photographed subject - do not be afraid to experiment!

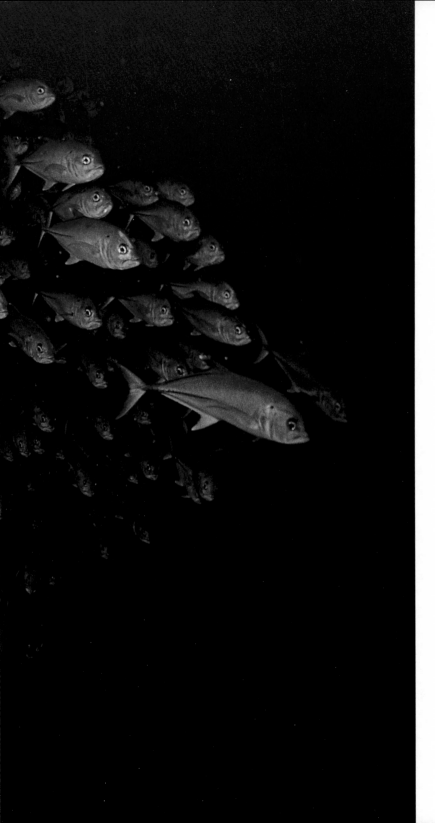

Mass and movement blend with unstoppable energy bursting towards the viewer - a lucky shot, taken hovering in midwater without breathing and waiting till the last second - when a large school of Bigeye trevallies *Caranx sexfasciatus* rushed towards me at full speed. The trick here is shooting at the last moment, when the onrushing school splits to avoid hitting the diver. Careful continuous focusing in Single Servo mode is obviously a must. Fritz Lang's *Metropolis* (inset) is a great filmic tutorial to the dynamic use of masses.

Guest
Photographer

Stephen
WONG

Hong Kong

Nikonos RS
Nikonos 20-35mm
ambient light

A beautiful, dynamic portrait of a pod of speeding Atlantic spotted dolphins *Stenella frontalis* taken by Stephen Wong - a great side portrait shot in close proximity to the surface. This simple, basically monochromatic yet quite striking image - shot with available ambient light - is greatly embellished by the long horizontal trails of bubbles leaving the streamlined mammals, which subconsciously suggest high speed and in doing so add a wonderful sense of urgency to the scene. Try envisioning the same photo without those swirling bubbles and you'll soon see the difference such small details can make.

Guest
Photographer

Alex
MUSTARD

United Kingdom

Nikon D100
Nikon 105mm
Subal housing
Subtronic Alpha dual strobes

Usually restricted to macro work, the venerable and much-loved Nikon 105mm (or any equivalent lens) can be put to good use when attempting "tele-macro" - shooting unapproachable subjects at a distance in very clear water. Alex Mustard demonstrates what can be achieved by careful use of this technique with this striking Red Sea portrait of a Red snapper *Lutjanus bohar*, winner of the BBC Wildlife Photographer of the Year in 2005 for its category. Notice how the extremely restricted depth of field offered by this lens at such distances has been taken advantage of by Alex to have his menacing subject in the foreground stand out from the school in the background.

— they may be pointing in the wrong direction, have the wrong settings, be off when you want them on or the exact opposite, and when taking photographs close to the surface in open water you shouldn't always expect to immediately realize there something's wrong with your equipment. So, once more, teach yourself to check and re-check constantly your camera gear and your strobes' settings while underwater — it's very easy, even for experienced photographers, to forget having reset something for a special occasion and then going back to normal shooting without changing back to the original set-up. Once more, it all goes back to the basic concept already expressed in the previous chapters — know your tools and learn to use them well, practice constantly until

Shooting at a distance can occasionally offer interesting results if composition is creative. In this image - shot with a 20mm at f.8 off the island of Walea in Northern Sulawesi - the strobe's flash was used to highlight the colorful sponge in the foreground, keeping the swirling tornado of jacks in the back. A touch of the flash can be seen being reflected by the jacks' silvery sides.

settings become a second nature and above all try to achieve that blissful state of mind in which physical and mental relaxation are perfectly balanced with a readiness to act rapidly and instinctively. A default TTL setting, in this respect, can arguably often help in automatically correcting minor aperture mistakes – but up to a point, and in any case you still have to check it's on, while post-production image-manipulating softwares like Photoshop and the like won't be able to save a badly framed picture - no matter how hard you may try. The large memory cards now available for digital cameras do not constrain us to the 36-frames limit of film cameras, allowing us more chances to correct mistakes – provided you realize you've been making those mistakes in the first place.

A panorama of beauty and colors - the endless palette of the coral reefs in Northern Sulawesi. The strobe's light adds a welcome highlight to the bright red sponge in the foreground, but it is the silhouetted Hawksbill turtle *Eretmochelys imbricata* in the upper background, swimming freely to the open blue ocean, which obviously defines the shot. The possibility of shooting at high apertures (from f.8 to f.16) offered by fish-eyes and wide-angles greatly increases depth of field and facilitates having every part of the final image in sharp focus, letting the photographer free to concentrate on composition.

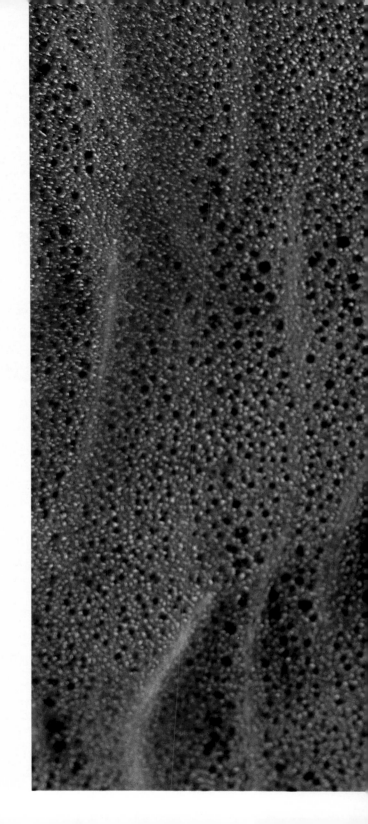

MACRO MAGIC
A boundless universe of opportunities

- The joys of macrophotography
- Correct techniques and equipment
- Choose your backgrounds
- Abstracts
- The fine art of spotting

Underwater microphotography is for connoisseurs – like a great vintage *Sauternes*, it requires atmosphere, relaxed concentration, good taste, some experience and a degree of sophistication. It also needs the highest dedication – as I am fond of repeating, it is not easy spending most of your dive with your nose a few inches away from the muck searching for horrid critters while the other divers in your boat are happily frolicking out there in the blue with dolphins, eagle rays and whale sharks. However, we've long been enthusiastic advocates of macro photography, and we know very well that back home it will be your photos of incredibly weird and impossibly colourful little subjects which, after all, will elicit the excited whoops of pure delight from your audience.

This is what macrophotography is all about - dazzling colors, unexpected patterns and textures, striking backgrounds, strange and usually overlooked small subjects. This two-centimeters long Yellow-lip triplefin *Helcogramma gymnauchen* perched on a powder-blue sponge in Pulau Lankayan has it all - plus a good dose of that undefinable "cuteness" factor which is often found on very small fish and which makes them so endearing to the casual viewer.

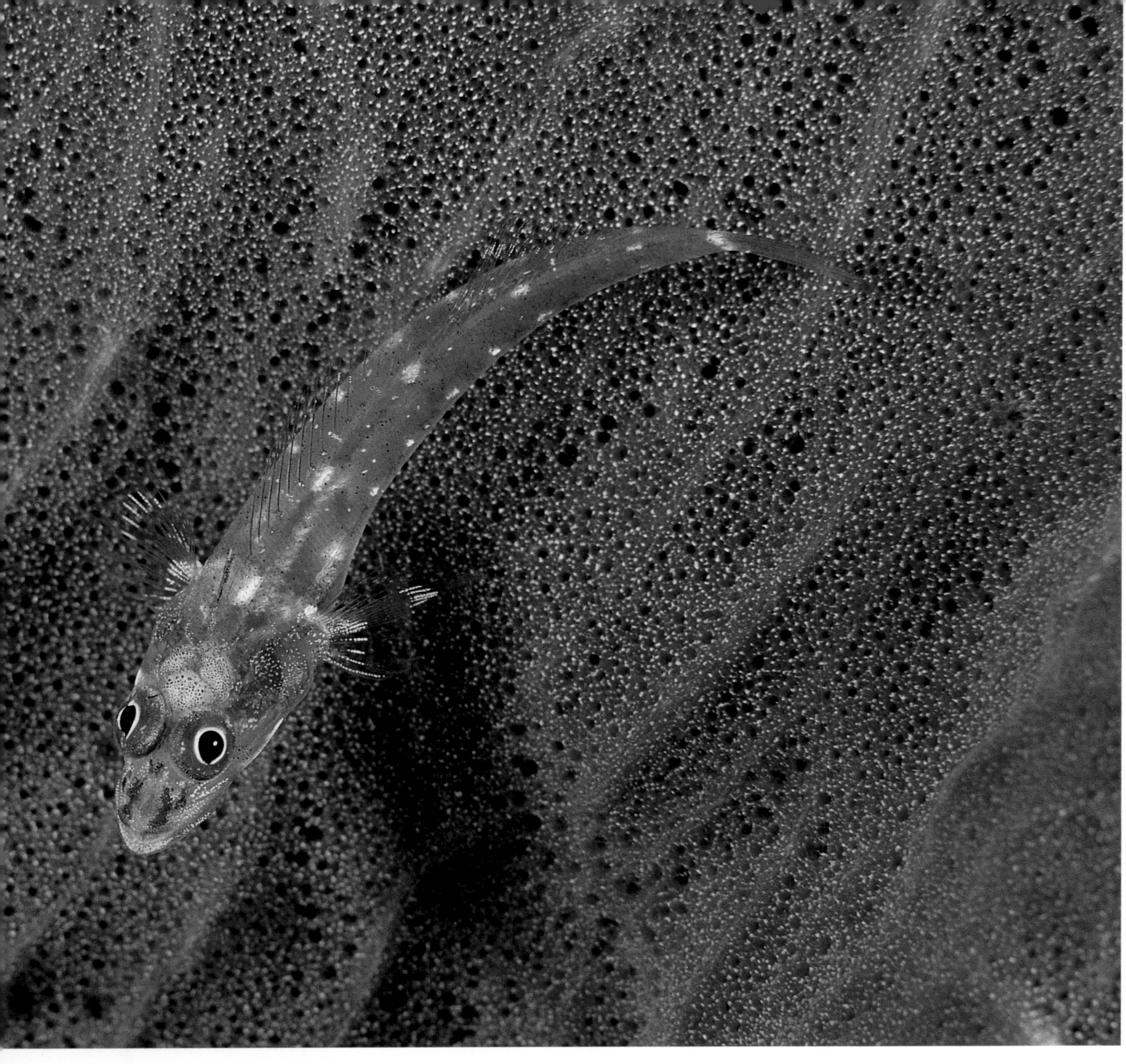

An impish, neon-lit Blue-ring octopus *Hapalochlaena lunulata* brightly flashes its aposematic, colorful livery warning predators of its deadly neurotoxic bite at Puri Jati, Bali. In macrophotography high f-stops (from f.16 to f.32 depending on their size) are mandatory to obtain good depth of field and sharpness of focus on every part of the camera subjects, most of which are of exceedingly small size. Lenses generally used are almost exclusively 60mm macro or 105mm macro, capable of 1:1 magnification.

A good example of the great importance of backgrounds in macrophotography - here the portrait of this tiny, colorful goby is wonderfully enriched by the rich geometry of the coral polyps cups on which it was found. Semi-abstract portraits on highly structured backgrounds such as this one call for shots taken from vertically above - one of the rare instances in underwater photography when this technique is actually advisable. Such naturally richly textured images do not really need enhancement by side-lighting effects.

Macro photography is usually an acquired taste, slowly developed after one has long been satiated with reef panoramas and big blue water stuff – but it is a taste which won't easily relinquish its grip on dedicated photographers. It offers endless opportunities – it's almost impossible running out of subjects or not finding interesting ones even on the most desolate stretches of rubble. It usually takes place at shallow depths and in calm water and is basically is the only type of underwater photography which can be undertaken during night diving (most - not quite correctly in fact - actually think of it as an exclusively nocturnal activity). It can also be practiced with overcast skies and rainy weather when wide-angle would be significantly compromised. It's easily accessible

A tiny semi-transparent commensal goby peeks at the approaching lens port from the safe refuge of its spun-sugar soft coral abode. Searching for such small and well-camouflaged subjects requests much patience, very good eyes and a great attention to detail - not everybody is willing to spend the whole dive carefully searching for such unassuming subjects.

to senior divers who don't really enjoy braving raging currents. Moreover, it offers wonderful opportunities for learning and even to witness previously undocumented behaviour or discover unknown or undescribed species. Underwater macro photography will also force you to explore the limits of your creativity, from simply documenting what you see to creating fascinating abstracts from colourful patterns, pushing you to really *see* and not simply watch what is taking place before you, thus suggesting new options with framing and strobe positioning since most macro subjects are static or at least usually rather slow-moving. It can be a lot of fun to slowly check every nook and cranny of the coral reef, to purposefully scan every square inch of appar-

Black volcanic sand bottoms represent some of the most desirable habitats for macro subjects, offering strongly contrasting backgrounds to photographers. Black-sand specimens like this beautiful Harlequin shrimp *Hymenocera elegans* feeding on a sea star at Seraya Secrets, in Bali, usually are more brightly colored than their white-sand counterparts.

Very clear water with little or no suspended particles offers interesting opportunities for "tele-macro", ie shooting from a relative distance unapproachable subjects using a 105mm macro lens as a tele. This sharp portrait of a Square-spot anthias *Pseudanthias pleurotaenia* - taken from a distance of about 150 centimeters at f.5.6 in Bunaken, Northern Sulawesi - shows the results which can be achieved. When employing this technique the strobe arms must be positioned as forward as possible to be able to light up the subject.

Another portrait of a goby on a highly textured background clearly shows the pitfalls of the minimal depth of field offered by macro lenses, even at high apertures. A straight from above composition was impossible for some reason - so great care was taken in getting the eyes of the tiny subject in the sharpest possible focus, in the knowledge that its rear part would be slightly out of focus. In such cases one has to go for the highest aperture, ie f.32, getting the strobes heads as close as possible to the subject - but even that is occasionally not enough.

ently deserted muck expanse, to carefully examine discarded rubbish supposedly devoid of life only to find weird and wonderful little fish faces peeking back at you, or grotesque cephalopods trying to slink away undetected, and amazingly colourful nudibranchs. In short, there is simply an infinite variety of macro critters waiting to be discovered. Can you remember the joy and satisfaction you felt when you found your first frogfish all by yourself? Well, that's what serious macro photography is all about after all – the simple joy of ever-renewed discovery.

To become a good underwater macro photographer you'll need to acquire a few specialist skills. One, which we have already examined in detail in the previous pages, is a

A Cockatoo waspfish *Ablabys taenianotus* portrait taken in the Lembeh Strait, Northern Indonesia, shows how lighting can affect close-ups. In this case the strobe on the right side of the subject was switched off to obtain sharper illumination from the other side, in the attempt to dramatize the sail-like appearance of its huge dorsal fin.

perfect control of your buoyancy – if you can't correctly float a few inches from your subjects you'll just break delicate corals, stir up zero-visibility silt storms in no time and in general make a mess for yourself (and others). Even learning to quietly lie down on a soft muck bottom without ruining your photographic chances is an art in itself – crashing down like a collapsing Zeppelin will scare away every small critter in the vicinity, stir up clouds of fine sediment which will take eternities to settle and present you with good chances of skewering yourself on the venomous spines of a devil scorpionfish or, even worse, a stonefish lying in ambush under the sand. So control your breathing and above all move your fins as little as possible. Be also considerate to other

Another attempt at creative lighting - an atmospheric vertical portrait of a Painted frogfish *Antennarius pictus* in which the light only comes from the strobe positioned below the subject. Such lighting techniques offer the most interesting results when used with subjects with strongly structured, expressive "facial" features.

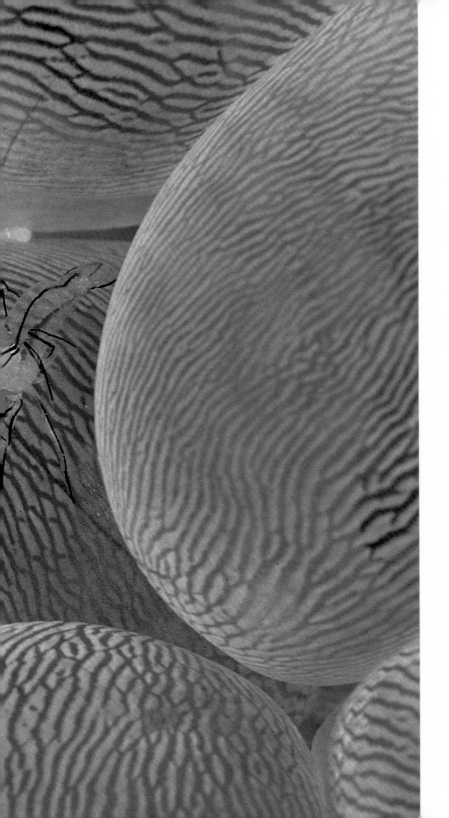

An even, soft lighting enhances the dreamy, truly otherwordly atmosphere pervading this portrait of a pair of Bubble coral shrimp *Vir philippinensis* found on - well, where else? - their Bubble coral *Pleurogyra sinuosa* home. The larger female is apparently carrying eggs. Macrophotography often offers the chance of getting striking images from very common and easily overlooked subjects, as in this case.

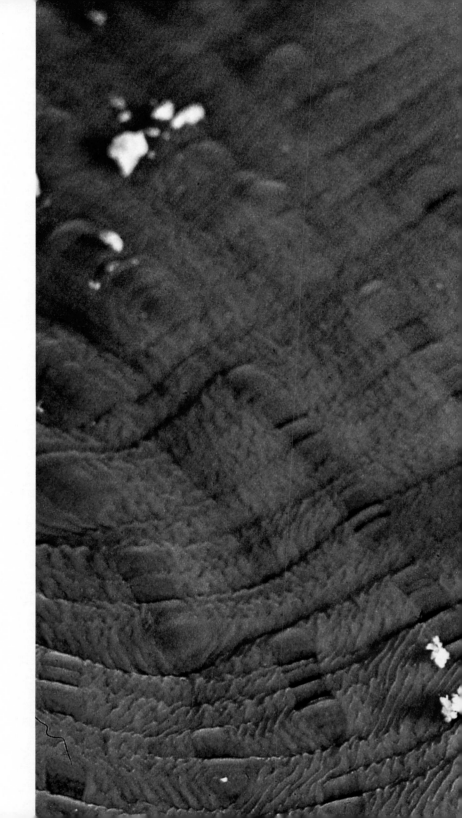

Another very common Indo-Pacific subject - a commensal cleaner shrimp *Periclemenes tosaensis* -gets the royal treatment when framed on the almost fluorescent, velvety mantle of its sea anemone host. Once again, the accent here is on incredibly bright colors and a pleasant composition - there appears to be no need to enhance the image with strong sideways lighting. Notice however how this - and most other subjects by the authors in this chapter - are framed more or less diagonally to add interest to the composition. particularly when plain backgrounds are present.

240

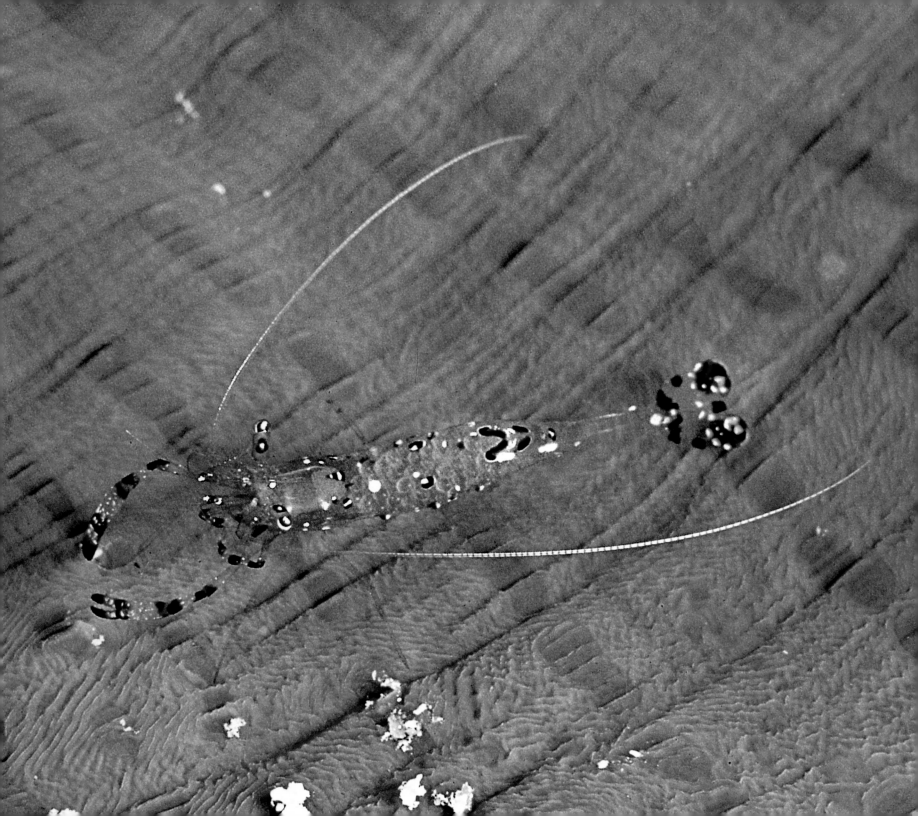

photographers and don't leave kicking up a blinding storm just because you've finished with those Harlequin shrimps! Doing good macro work also involves a lot of studying – you are seldom going to bump into your tiny subjects by pure chance (even if many will just be conspicuously sitting in the open, like most nudibranchs – which being toxic advertise their noxiousness wearing aposematic bright liveries), so you'll have to teach yourself what lives where, and how they act and react within their environment. Some subjects are quite fearless (clownfish will actually attack underwater photographers – being nibbled by an irate one can be quite startling) while others will simply drive you nuts at your first frustrated attempts to get a decent photo of them. Most wary, shy subjects will generally get used to a static or slow-moving diver soon enough, however, so then it's just a matter of being still and enjoying the opportunity of closely watching their behaviour before trying to move in – garden eels and shrimp gobies, for instance, will occasionally allow a very close approach if one is patient enough. The question you have to ask yourself is, are you interested enough in this to spend 40 minutes of your precious dive time hardly moving at all? I use low-volume respirations while lying on the sand to slowly inch my way forward towards them, all the while keeping the camera housing glued to my mask – you'll have to learn to become part of the submerged panorama, listening to your regulator hiss for company and squinting out of the corner of your eye to check

A sideways portrait of a Striped triplefin *Helcogramma striata* makes a bold chromatic statement even if the coral head the little fish is perched on is really nothing to shout about. When backgrounds are rather listless - as in this case - it is often advisable to concentrate on the subject itself, leaving creative composition temporarily aside and focusing on its inherent qualities instead. In this occasion the bright metallic "roadster finish" of the tiny fish and its curiously jutting lower jaw were considered enough to justify a try.

A small, colorful, casual collection of basslets, blennies, dottybacks and damselfish clearly shows the wonderful results which can be obtained when adopting "tele-macro" to portray small, active and above all very shy subjects. Users of digital cameras are greatly facilitated in the use of this technique, since low strobe output and a generally higher sensitivity to light levels allows shooting extremely alert, sensitive species from greater distances without spooking them. Lower strobe output also means much faster recharging and almost no backscatter in less than optimal visibility, a great bonus when photographing in coastal waters.

Chapter 6 • MACRO MAGIC

245

A metallic shrimp goby *Amblyeleotris latifasciata* shows how incredibly colorful some "muck diving" species can be - this and several other very striking species are exclusively found on shallow, barren silt or sand bottoms. Getting close enough to these very shy animals is an interesting exercise in self-control, patience and air consumption by itself - but the results can often be remarkably satisfying. The advent of digital cameras has made such undertakings easier, since the original 105mm once used on film actually becomes a 130mm when used in conjunction with most digital camera sensors available at the moment.

A study in deception - blending to perfection with its coral rubble background, a Clown frogfish *Antennarius maculatus* successfully pretends to be an encrusted sponge in the Lembeh Strait, Northern Sulawesi. Underwater macrophotography offers interesting chances to observe and learn about marine species behavior - in fact it requests learning to allow subsequent observation. Once more, an even diffused lighting from the sides and slightly above is more than enough to make justice to this weird and wonderful subject.

what's happening around you. With many other subjects, frustration will often be inevitable– I personally find flasher wrasses the most frustrating subjects of all with their frantic, demented, high-speed flitting a few feet above the bottom, all the time keeping a constant distance from you (despite all your efforts to get closer) and the tantalising displaying of their maddeningly colourful, streaming dorsal fins. Whatever you do, always remember not to harm or roughly handle your subjects. Gentle manipulation with the use of that essential tool, a metal pointing stick, is to be accepted and expected when needed – there's nothing wrong in gently and temporarily flushing a dwarf lionfish from hiding, or waving some sand away to uncover the grotesque death's head grin of a

The bottom of a Pincushion seastar *Culcita novaeguineae* offers a striking abstract, somehow subconsciously inspired by the extravagantly coreographed musical numbers of Busby Berkeley's *Footlight Parade*.

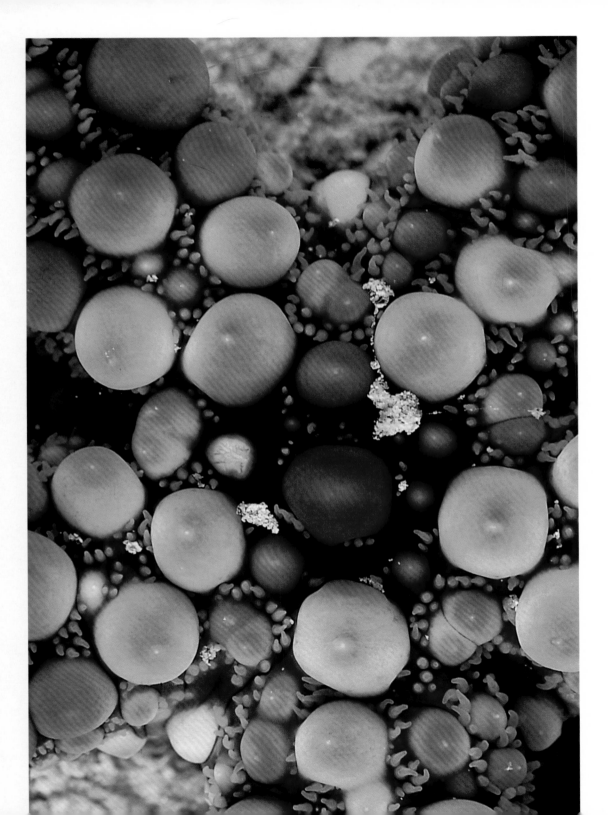

dug-in stargazer. However, it's absolutely damnable what lots and lots of divers (and too-eager-to-please dive guides) often do, i.e. catching small animals, grabbing them unceremoniously and carelessly dumping them somewhere just because the so-called photographer has decided they need a different background to look good in a picture. This is not only silly (most macro species are strictly habitat-specific so they'll look out of place in the final photograph) but also unethical (several macro commensals, such as featherstar squat lobsters, will soon die if separated from their species-specific host). The trick of herding several specimens together to get a "good" shot is also to be condemned, as is the bad habit of feeding or creating feeding situations with benthic

Another and slightly more conventional sea star - this time framed from directly above - offers another dazzling abstract.
Creative macrophotography truly offers the opportunity to really see for those who take it seriously.

Guest
Photographer

Takako
UNO

Hong Kong

Nikonos RS
Nikonos 50mm
Nikon SB104 + Sea & Sea YS30
strobes

Taking full advantage of the alien radial symmetry and the impossibly colorful tile-like patterns found on the bottom face of a Pincushion sea star *Culcita novaeguineae*, Takako Uno creates an arresting abstract - as if nature herself had been inspired the organic and the inorganic by the imaginative palette of a Klee or a Kandinsky.

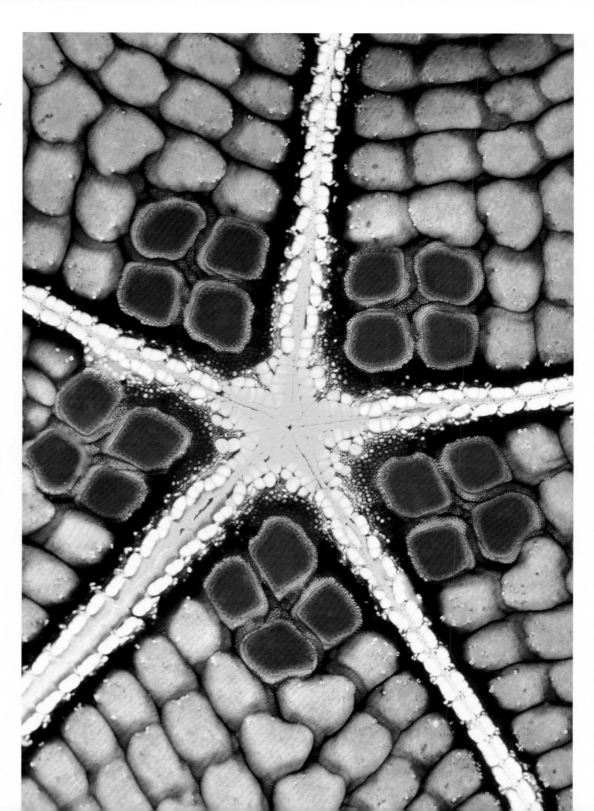

Guest
Photographer

Takako
UNO

Hong Kong

Nikonos RS
Nikonos 50mm
Sea & Sea YS120 + YS130 strobes

Another striking abstract, once again from Takako Uno - who creates colorful, neon-like radial patterns framing from directly above the dorsal surface of a highly venomous Fire urchin *Asthenosoma iji-mai*. With her image she successfully demonstrates here the most important quality for macrophotographers - being able to recognize beauty when one sees it.

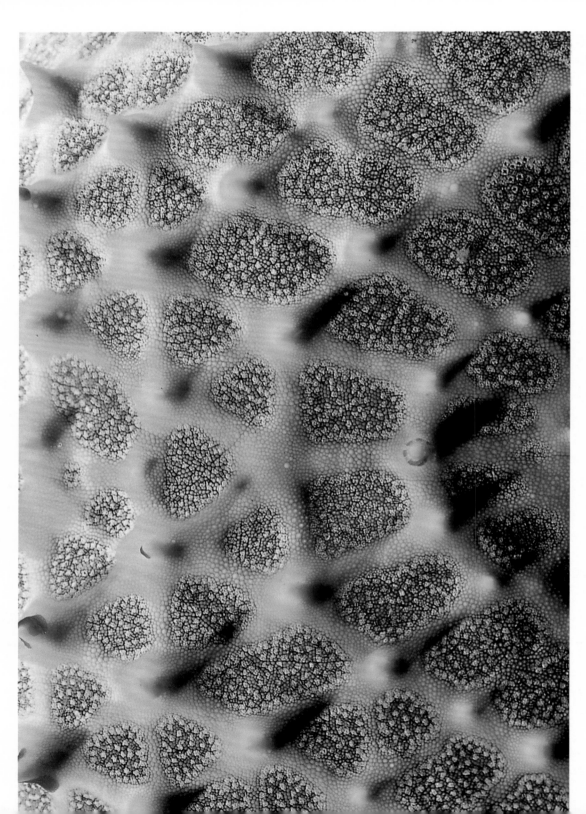

Guest
Photographer

Alan J. POWDERHAM

United Kingdom

Nikon F4
Nikon 105mm
Nexus housing
Nikon SB105 dual strobes

Seeing where most others would only simply blindly *watch*, Alan J.Powderham transforms the dorsal surface of a sea star into an alien landscape, lemon-yellow geometric, mysterious nipple-like cones rising in recurring rythms and patterns from a tightly decorated, frosted surface. Recognizing beauty and interest in the apparently mundane is one of the secrets of successful macrophotography - the capacity to show others, like a magician on a stage, what seemed invisibile and yet was there all the time for everybody to see.

GUEST PHOTOGRAPHER

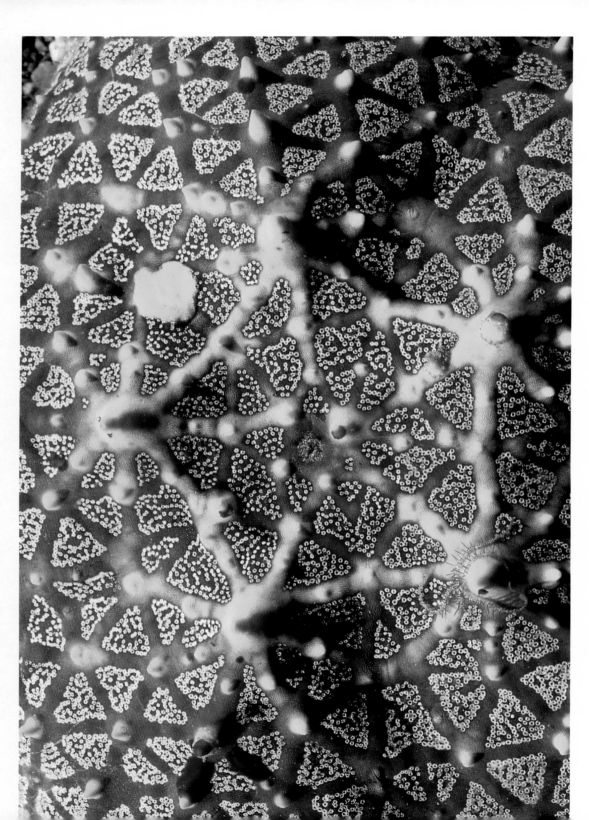

Guest
Photographer

Alan J.
POWDERHAM
United Kingdom

Nikon F4
Nikon 105mm
Nexus housing
Nikon SB105 dual strobes

Yet one more spectacular variation on the same humble sea star theme, this time taking the appearance of an extraterrestrial network of mysteriously connected highways, a fractal-like weaving of unknown psychedelic geometries evoking the magic of numbers. Patterns which endlessly repeat themselves, and yet endlessly vary from one specimen to the other, always changing and at the same time remaining constant to the parameters of the species - enough to invoke wonder, and amazement, in the eyes of the beholder.

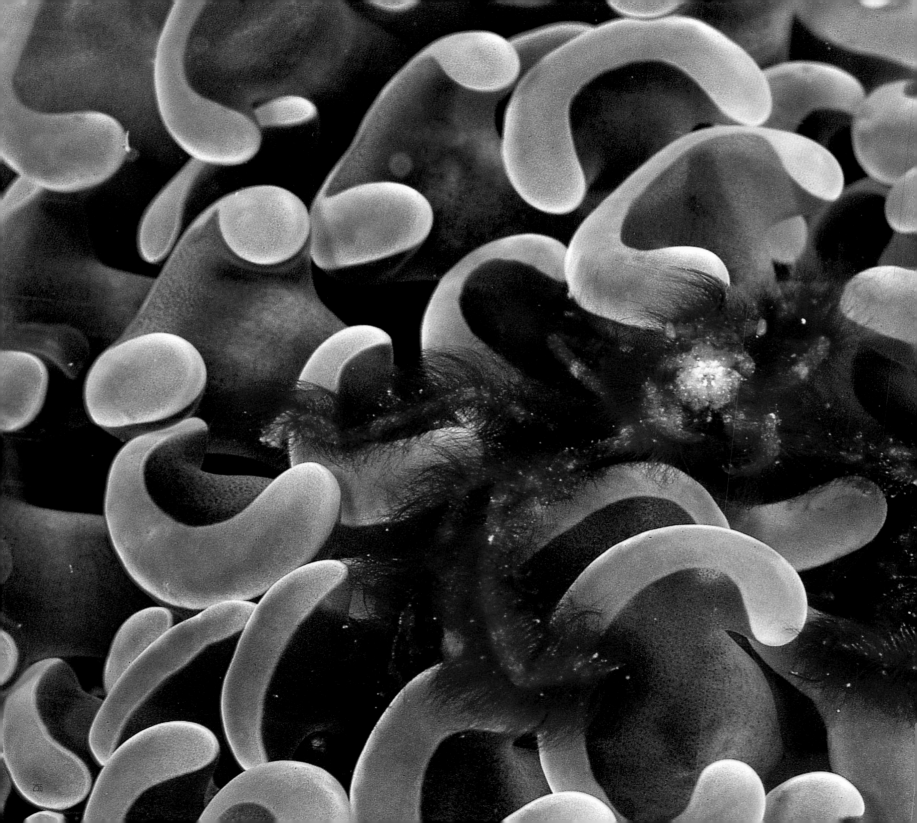

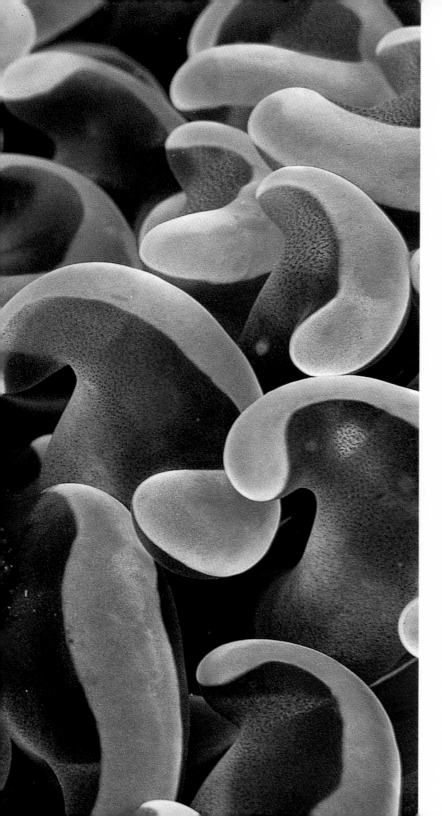

Perched among its coral host polyps, a fierce-looking Orangutan crab *Achaeus japonicus* glares like a miniature gargoyle at the onlooker, its hair-like reddish growth waving in the current, the red brightness of its eyes lit up by the strobes'flash. Yet one more good example of the graphic importance of textured backgrounds in macro images - not a problem in this case, as this species in often found on such a queer-looking host, the kidney-shaped polyps of *Euphyllia ancora* corals.

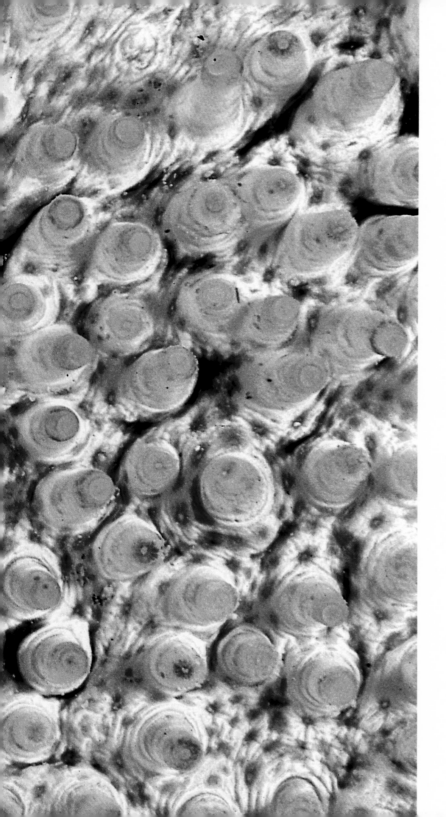

Tightly dug-in in close proximity to its sea cucumber host's anus - a readily if not exactly endearing accessible source of constantly flowing nutrients - a commensal crab *Lissocarcinus orbicularis* offers a study in chromatic contrast as it sits in a riot of colors and highly textured shapes. Appearing underwater to the naked eye as a jumble of greys and muted browns, this techicolored organic landscape is a good example of the need to learn about marine species and their actual colors before trying to actually photograph them underwater.

predators such as frogfish to obtain that pathetic, supposedly "lucky" feeding shot. Nature needs no such ludicrous special effects to show its beauty, and the performance of a photographer actually tricking himself into the conviction of having taken a great shot is a sad sight indeed. You weren't good, you just cheated.

Close-up macro photography is strictly dependant on artificial lighting, offering interesting possibilities of creative control via the positioning of strobes and the different setting of f-stops, which in turn regulate depth of field. We usually go for naturalistic, descriptive images, so we tend to position our strobes slightly above the horizontal and about 45° degrees towards the subject, generally setting at f.22 or

Night dives usually offer wonderful opportunities for striking macro images. Coral polyps are usually fully open and feeding on plankton which is drifting by in the water column - a great chance to create interesting abstracts. Always use high aperture settings (f.22 or even f.32 in extreme cases) to achieve the greatest depth of field.

even f.32 with very small subjects to obtain maximum depth of field, but nothing forbids you to experiment with different solutions, such as creative backlighting (see-through effects with semi-transparent subjects such as soft corals or silhouettes with small fish). Autofocus is also a great asset for us, since we seem to have never experienced the difficulties encountered by others while using this wonderfully convenient technology – in fact, from what we see, hand focusing in macro photography usually results in a distinctive lack of sharpness and frequent slightly out-of-focus images which might have otherwise been perfect. Just remember to always focus on the subject's eyes – if it has any. Generally speaking, we believe the best results are those taken keep-

Some coral polyps will be fully open and feeding, emerging from their cups, even during the day - another good opportunity for interesting abstracts when other, more challenging subjects are temporarily amiss. Coral polyps are extremely variable in color and shape - it's quite easy ending up building a collection of shots of them.

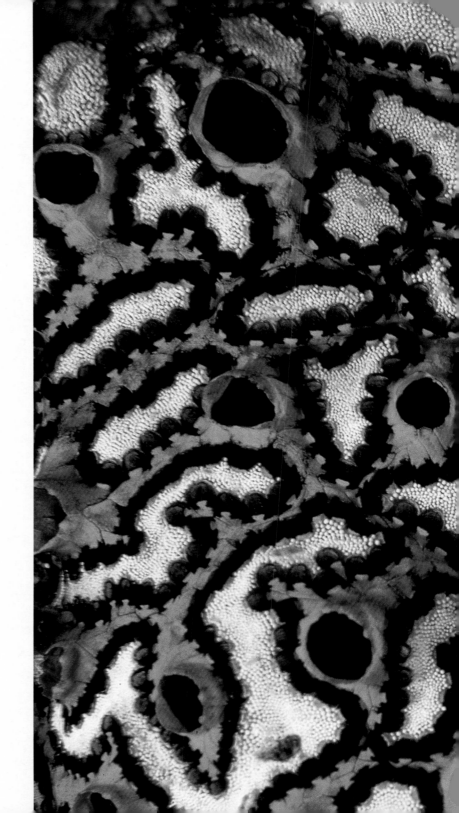

Not an aerial panorama from another planet, but a two-centimeter square detail from the surface of a Botryllid colonial ascidian, an encrusting organism occasionally observed on rocks and deads corals in the Sulawesi Sea. Being a good macro photographer above all means being able to immediately recognize interesting - and occasionally downright unique - subjects among the confusing jumble of the coral reef, never dismissing them as too plain or common: in more than 1.000 dives all over the world we have observed this species only once.

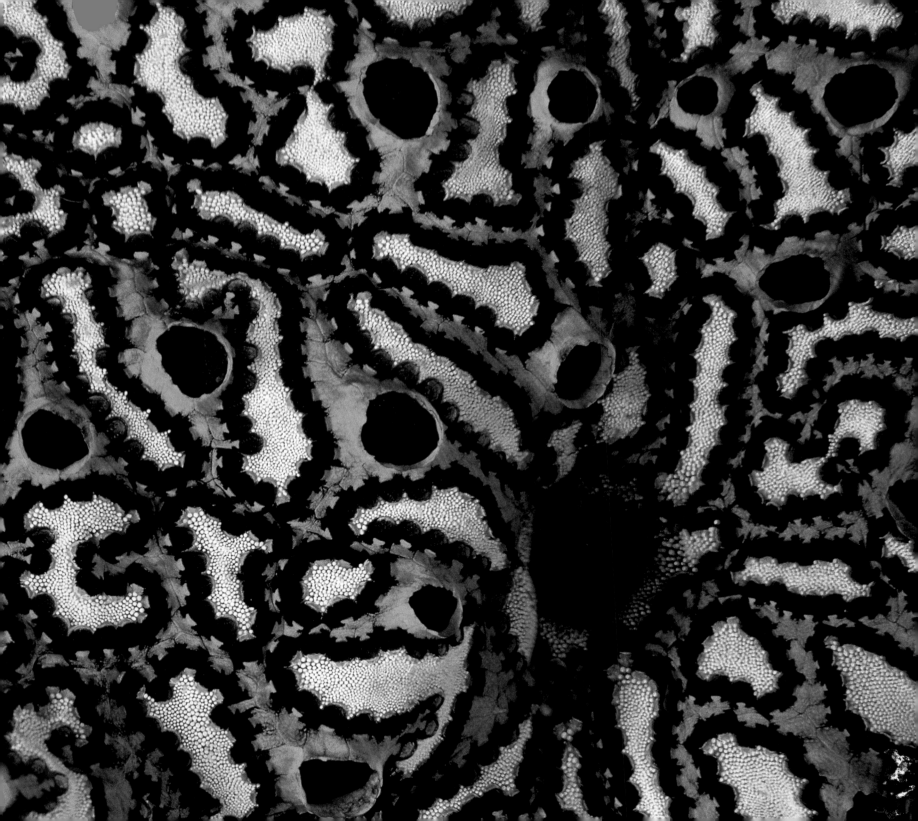

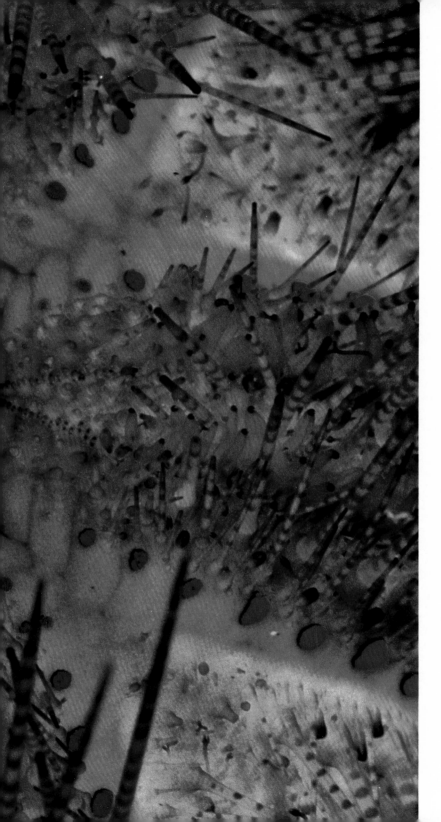

"The Zebra Crab from Hell" rises out of the murky bottoms of the Lembeh Strait in Northern Indonesia, its tiny crustacean body clinging by means of specially-modified back legs to the dorsal surface of a boiling lava-like sea urchin. An arresting image - despite the fact that its fiery background, looking like a veritable furnace of hell, appears a muted brown underwater, revealing its neon-like glow only when lit by the artificial light of the photographer's strobes. Nature - especially in the macro realm - can be quite deceptive to the casual observer.

ing the subject at the observer's level, or even from slightly below: shots from directly above will only work in a few specific instances and when looking for deliberate creative effects, such as with spread-armed small octopi (interesting radial look) or tiny gobies lying on coral heads (geometric, structured patterns). Again, feel free to experiment and try new perspectives – some of the examples featured among this book's guest contributors galleries clearly and brilliantly contradict our theories, showing that fresh, unfettered creativity will always result in interesting and occasionally arresting images. However, there's one aspect generally shared by most good macro images which strive to achieve some aesthetic quality beyond being merely descriptive, and that is the background against which the subject has been photographed. As underwater photographers, we are particularly lucky in this respect – macro backgrounds can vary from the velvety, spun-sugar nuances on anemone surfaces to the glassy, jewel-like ones of soft corals, to the hard geometric patterns offered by gorgonians and hard corals. Even bare sand – particularly black volcanic one – can be used to good effect to maximize the interesting visual effect offered by strange body shapes and unorthodox colour patterns. A flamboyant cuttlefish would not look as interesting if portrayed among a confusing jumble of corals, for example. Once more, let me repeat myself – this does not mean grabbing a small yellow frogfish and sticking it on a purple sponge because you think the colour contrast will be inter-

Emperor partner shrimp *Periclemenes imperator* inhabit the dorsal surface of large nudibranchs and sea cucumbers, but they are rarely sighted as such a perfectly positioned and gaudily colored pair - even if this image could probably benefit from some careful cropping on the right side. Macro photographers should always refrain from "posing" their subjects by force or artificially arranging behavioral shots. Taking full advantage of chance encounters is much more satisfactory and usually offers better results - an experienced eye immediately recognizes artificially created feeding or posed shots anyway.

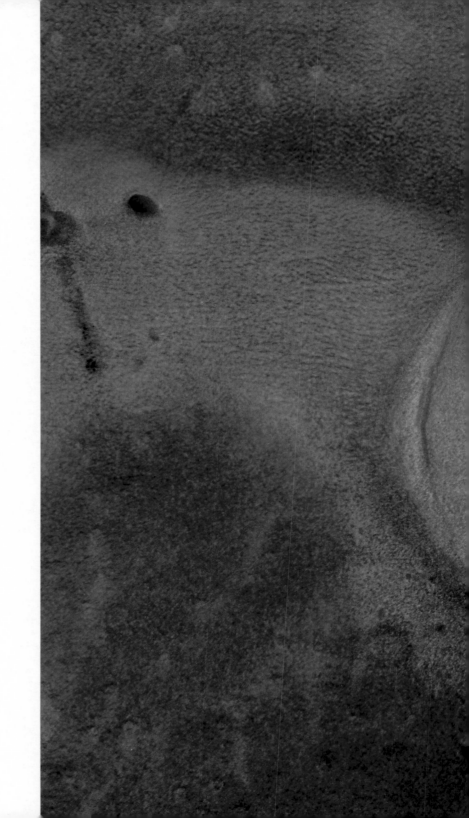

The ideal training ground for aspiring macro photographers, shallow reefs
at night offer good chances of observing and closely approaching
sleeping parrotfish, usually tucked in among the corals and rather
unwilling to move away if not directly harassed.
Their dazzlingly colorful liveries offer a wide choice of abstracts - from
close-ups of the eyes as in this case, to scale or mouth details.
Care must always be taken not to overly disturb the resting animals,
leaving them immediately alone at the first signs of stress.

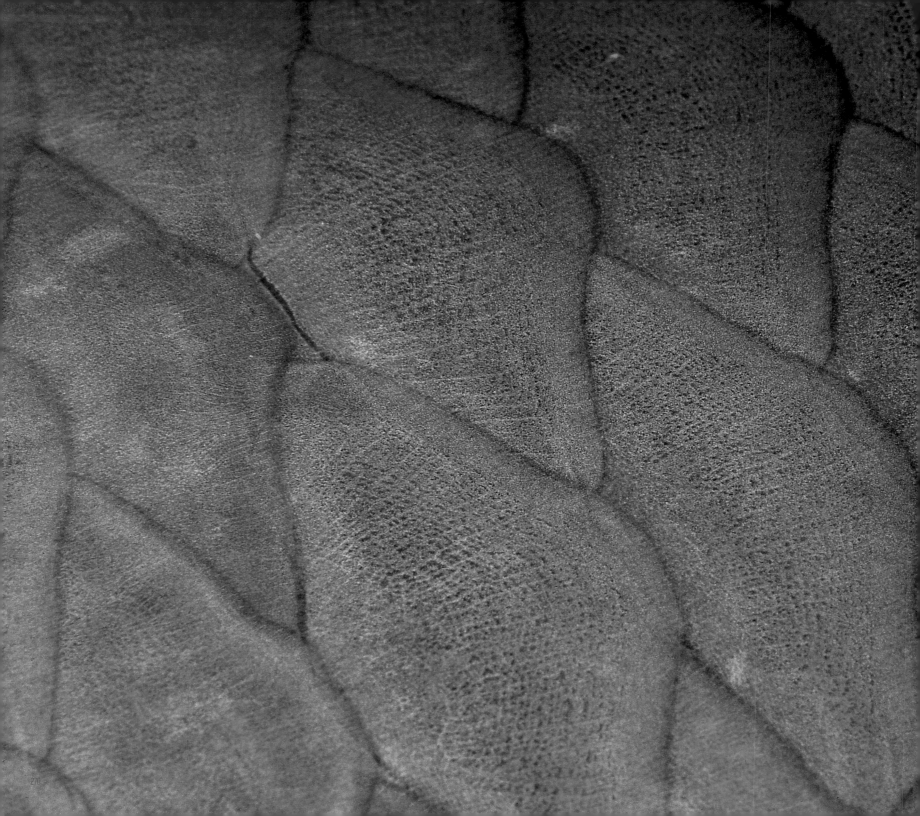

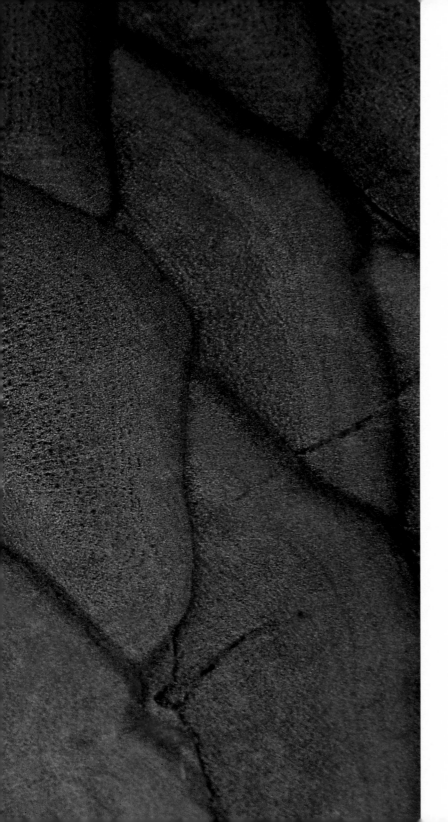

The finely sculpted surfaces and dazzling coloration of parrotfish scales usually offer great chances for abstracts, allowing the observation of details usually invisible to the naked eye. Most diurnal fish tend to radically change their colors and patterns when they rest among the corals at night, occasionally giving rise to confusion in identification when photographed. When doing macro photography on coral reefs at night it is of the utmost importance to carefully and constantly check buoyancy and positioning to avoid damage to the surrounding fragile coral colonies.

esting – quite the opposite: it will look awful and it will look wrong. Picking the right, interesting backgrounds means instead to instantly recognize the opportunity offered by chance, to appreciate the possibilities offered by luck – to see a work of art in a small jewelled shrimp hovering above a softly-hued anemone, or in a tiny blenny peeking out of a hole bored in a coral colony, and to transform that opportunity into a great photograph. If it's not backgrounds, it's in the choice of subjects: macro photographers rightfully delight in the horrifying, the weird, the grotesque, and the highly unusual. The realm of macro is of the monstrous and the bizarre. The fixed mad stare of a grinning stargazer, the death's head monstrous looks of a stonefish, the jagged-ragged

Less than colorful subjects can offer good opportunities for fascinating abstracts anyway - as it has happened with this extreme close-up of a Mushroom coral *Fungia* sp. showing its water-flow optimization channels. A very common and generally overlooked species, again, which however proves being of great photographic interest if observed without preconceived notions.

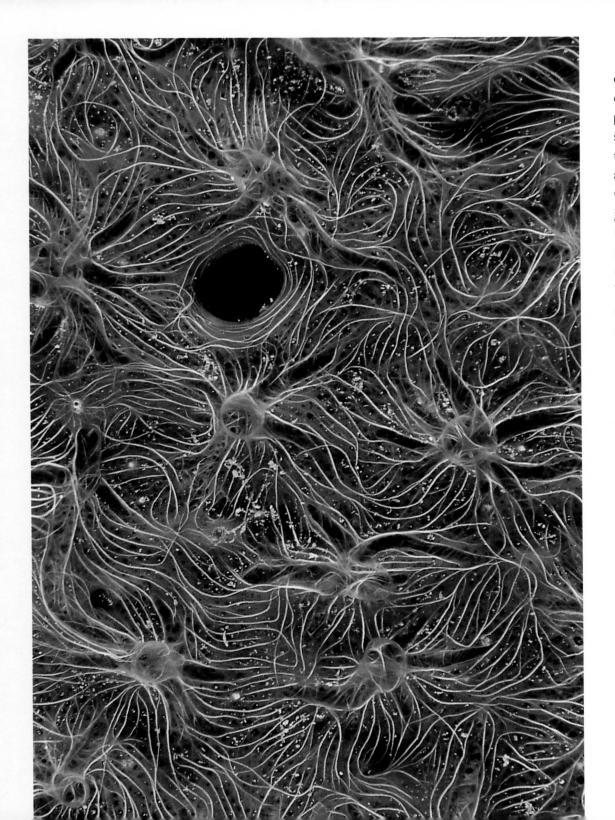

dragging of a devil scorpionfish, the devilish glare of an ambushing scorpionfish, the bloated sponge-like shape of a frogfish — all conspire in their horrid, strange beauty to create wonderful, fascinating images. Once more, most of the fun and joy lies in recognizing beauty — feeling one with it, with nature itself — right where it lies, freely and simply offered for us to admire and enjoy. This is — as a good friend of ours aptly puts it — the central art of seeing.

Being able to see, to identify and recognize beautiful and interesting subjects, will also sooner or later tempt you to explore the mesmerizing realm of pure abstracts — extreme close-ups of shapes or colour patterns (fins, eyes, scale details) in which the real identity of

Another exceptionally common and generally overlooked species - the purple encrusting sponge *Nara nemathifera* of the Indo Pacific - suddenly reveals a sensuously woven pattern when photographed in close-up. Care was taken to correctly position the orifice in the sponge to balance an otherwise rather featureless composition.

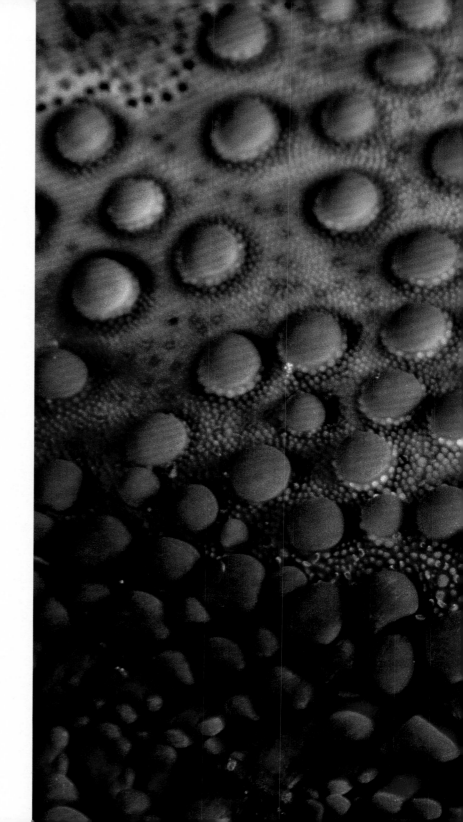

Could life on other, distant, alien planets look like this? A pair of exceedingly small and armored Partner shrimp *Periclemenes soror* cautiously tread the ventral surface of a Pincushion seastar *Culcita novaeguineae*, bathed in the orange and bright purple glow of a Martian twilight. The accurate portrayal of symbiotic relationships taking place between different marine species is one of the most enjoyable and satisfying aspects of underwater macrophotography.

the original subject actually fades away, giving way to pure, almost hallucinatory abstractions of light and hue. Again, this is a fine form of underwater photographic art by itself — possibly the most refined and sophisticated variation on the subject of underwater macro photography — which can occasionally give rise to truly dazzling images: one needs a special eye for it however, a deep spiritual and visual empathy with the subject which enables the artist to isolate and extrapolate a tiny detail from the general context in his own mind, long before committing to taking the shot. A well developed understanding of architecture or art would conceivably be useful when approaching these studies in structural abstraction. If you feel ready to give it a try, then it is best to

Close-up details of Giant clam *Tridacna* sp. can be incredibly sensuous and atmospheric - and yet these easily accessible subjects, commonly found in very shallow water on healthy coral reefs, are usually overlooked by most divers and photographers. Coming in all sorts of colors and patterns, they only require a careful approach to avoid them getting alarmed and closing up.

start with extreme, psychedelic close-ups of static, richly patterned and relatively large subjects. Indo-Pacific giant clams can provide a good initial choice, as are closely approachable sleeping parrotfish. Again, as with all macro photography, it all boils down to teaching oneself the difficult and rewarding art of truly *seeing*. Which, to be really effective, needs a good pair of experienced eyes – so never underestimate the usefulness of an expert local dive guide, especially if you're not blessed with Antonella's eagle sight, which has put many an experienced critter spotter to shame from Mabul to Lembeh!

It is true, as I said above, that you will have to learn to recognize beauty when you chance upon it, but at the same time it cannot also be denied that local knowledge of

Detail of the syphon of a Giant clam *Tridacna* sp. in extreme close-up, showing its beautiful iridescent colors and patterns. These large bivalves are extremely sensitive to sudden variations in water pressure and light levels - the only way to approach them very closely is to slowly "float over", being very careful not to cast a shadow over them in the process.

Guest
Photographer

John
SCARLETT
USA

Nikon D2X
Nikon 105mm
Subal ND2 housing
Inon Z220S dual strobes

Fingered dragonets *Dactylopus dactylopus* are not the easiest of marine animals to approach up close, but John Scarlett has been able to get a wonderful portrait of one while diving in Komodo. Patience and perseverance usually pay off in macrophotography - notice the subtle variations in color, the fine detail on the skin surface and the bulging, transparent corneas which are only visible from a perfect frontal shot. The necessity of the removal of the substrate in the bottom part of the image - done in Photoshop in post-production - can be debated and is a matter of personal taste, but the black background doubtlessly and greatly enhances the colorful livery of this beautiful marine animal.

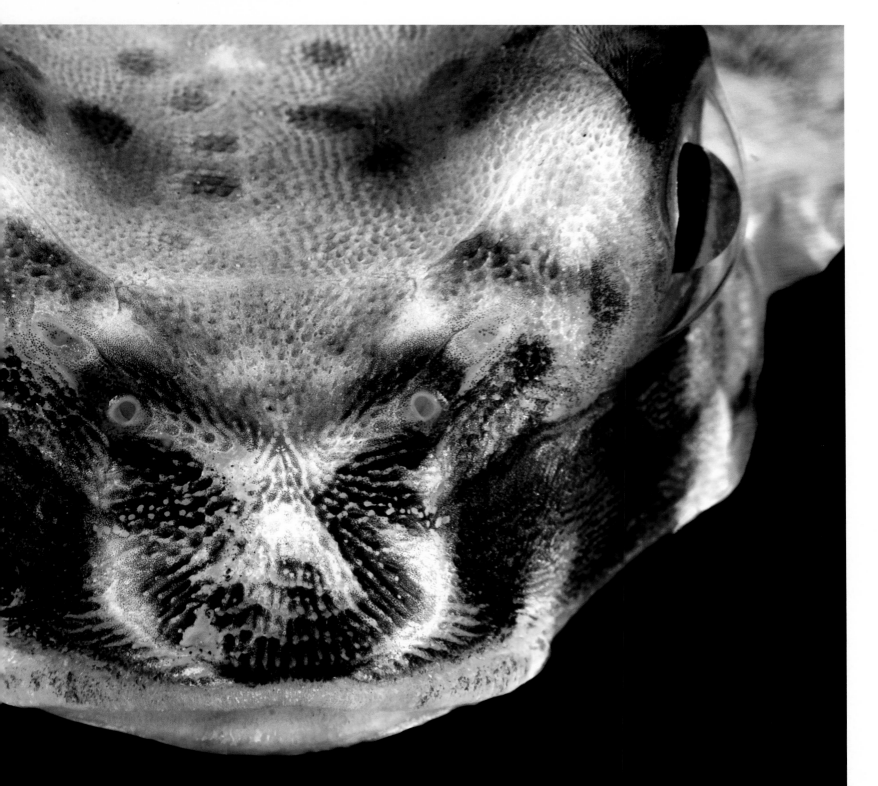

Pygmy seahorses - here a cream-and-strawberry *Hippocampus denise* in the waters off Kri Island in Raja Ampat, West Papua - are exceptionally tiny, rarely cooperative and much loved dwellers of a few Indo-Pacific gorgonian species. Given their ludicrously small size - some do not exceed 5mm in total length - and current-prone habitats, one has to rely on high f-stops (usually f.22 or f.32) to keep everything in focus. In several instances the resulting black background will contrast quite pleasingly with the branching sea fan colony, creating interesting patterns and helping in outlining the little creature's features.

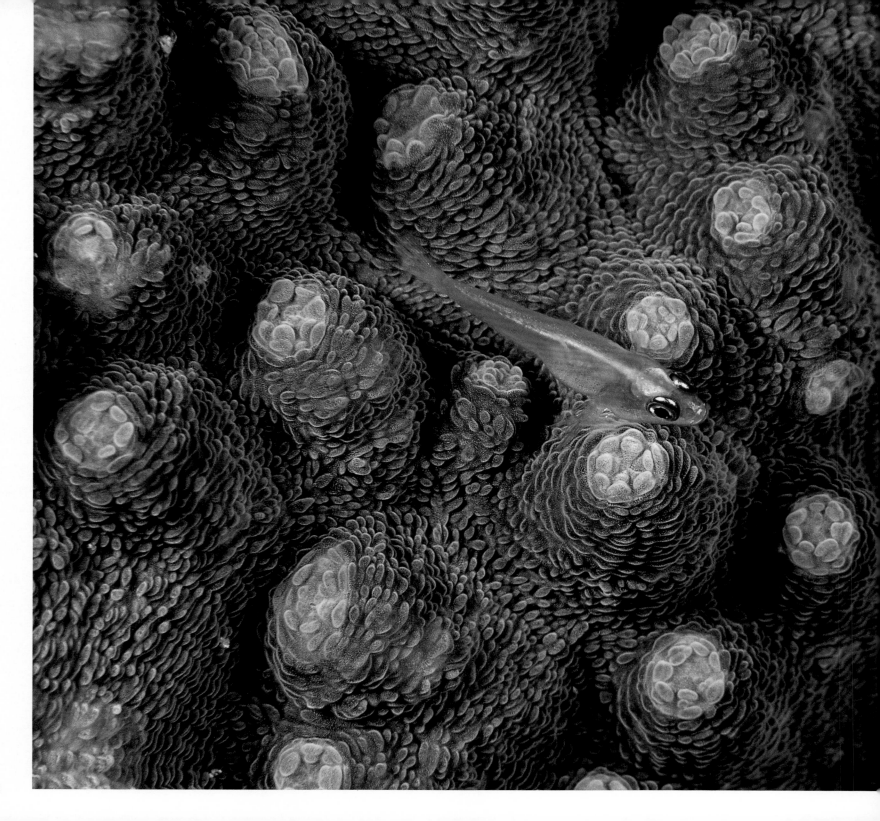

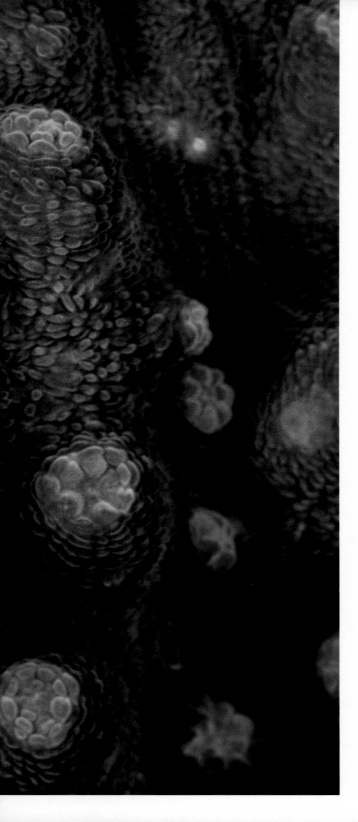

the habits and habitats of many small and not-so-small species will prove immensely helpful in obtaining good photographs. Not everybody is able to readily spot pygmy seahorses after all, so do not feel shy and ask your guide to help with finding specific subjects. You'll save yourself a lot of frustration, you'll be able to concentrate better and you'll be following a wonderful learning curve in process if you pay attention to what is going on instead of letting yourself be led around like sheep. You'll be amazed how quickly you'll learn to be able to find them yourself with a little field experience – Antonella now routinely locates notoriously well-camouflaged critters like leaf scorpionfish, blue-ring octopus and baby clown frogfish, often beating experienced dive guides to them. I'm not blessed with such wonderful eyesight, but at least I can rely on an invaluable spotter!

In this portrait of a tiny, quite colorful but rather nondescript goby perched on a coral head what actually catches the viewer's eye is not the fish itself but - for a change - the actual background instead, with its sci-fi movie alien planet-like mounds tipped by a bright "radioactive" fluorescent green coral polyp cups. The original subject of the image was in fact the fish, but something in the corals it was perching on must have tickled my imagination - a photographer's instinct at work, presumably. Planned or not, the result is interesting and pleasing to the eye - which is what counts.

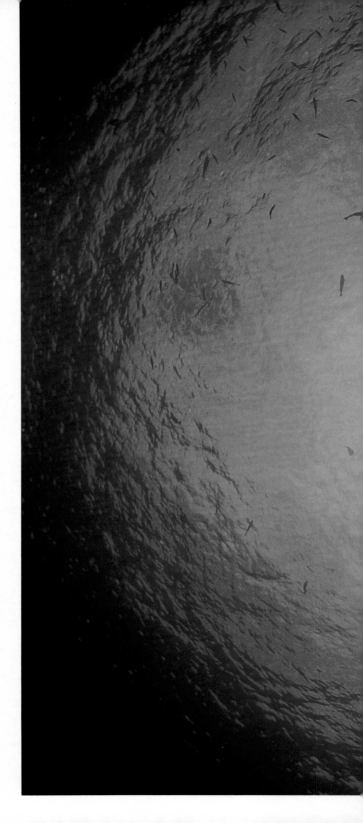

Chapter 7

WIDE ANGLE WONDERS
Completing the magic circle

- For starters and masters alike
- Correct techniques and equipment
- Wrecks
- Split Images
- Do's and Don'ts

The path leading to wide-angle photography is almost as circular as the spectacular images these lenses provide. Often enthusiastically adopted by beginners for their apparent ease of use, wide-angle and fish-eye lenses are usually re-discovered later on in their career by experienced photographers, often looking for a fresh challenge after years of fish portraits and the demanding requirements of macro photography. In truth, no other underwater image is appealing and exhilarating as that of a colourful, vibrant reef panorama at shallow depth, brightly lit by the slanting sun's rays – and this can generally only be achieved with the judicious use of a good wide-angle or fish-eye lens. While the correct use of the first (falling between 24mm and 18mm focal length)

Fish-eye underwater photography can appear deceptively easy to the untrained eye. Apparently of simple use to the beginner, panoramic lenses will only produce their best results- which can often be absolutely spectacular -when employed by experienced photographers who are familiar with their peculiar quirks. The most common mistake when using fish-eyes is shooting from too far away - this image of a male Green turtle *Chelonia mydas* swimming by Antonella in Sipadan, Malaysian Borneo, was taken at f.8 with the animal's belly almost grazing the big 16mm dome.

offers no real challenges as long as some basic rules are followed, that of fish-eyes (falling between 16mm and 10.5mm focal length) is rather more demanding due to the inherent deformation of the horizon and corners imposed by such extreme lenses. General-use wide-angle lenses also require the fitting of rather small and manageable domes on underwater camera housings, while the huge ones often required for fish-eyes can prove occasionally challenging and even fatiguing to divers unaccustomed to managing the high positive buoyancy resulting from the increased amount of trapped air. Several current wide-angle lenses available on the market today – created for digital cameras - are also available as zooms (such as the formidable Nikon 12-24mm), offering added

Another Green turtle *Chelonia mydas*, here quietly resting on Sipadan's reef and once more with Antonella posing in the background. Notice the diffuse, even lighting given by the widely spread twin strobes, the slight deformation at the lower corners - typical of fish-eyes - and the perfect stance of the model.

flexibility underwater and reduced luggage weight while sacrificing nothing in image quality. This is a significant consideration regarding restrictions imposed on flight baggage nowadays. Moving from general-use wide-angles to the extremes of fish-eyes is natural progression, so sooner or later you'll be challenging yourself (and your financial resources) with a short, stubby lens and a very big, very buoyant panoramic dome. These are offered in optical-grade coated glass or high grade plastics, and despite the professionals' obvious and much-touted preference for the former, we are convinced excellent results can be obtained using the latter. Optical-grade glass fish-eye domes are very heavy, dangerously fragile, easily scratched (despite being often promoted as

A small school of Tallfin batfish *Platax teira* swims by Antonella at Mike's Point, Raja Ampat, West Papua. Notice the graceful, dynamic stance of the model - swimming at full speed despite the ungainly extra camera she's carrying - and the above-water vegetation clearly visible through Snell's window behind her.

scratch-resistant) and extremely expensive – once scratched, more-over, they're more or less ruined and will need a major overhaul as the damage will be visible in the final photograph due the optical proper-ties of glass. Lexan or polycarbonate fish-eye domes - which we have always used and which we'll keep on using in the future – are much lighter, almost indestructible, much more economical and above all perfectly usable even when lightly scratched, as seawater filling the groove will virtually cancel it from the finished photograph. We have also heard of a photographer absent-mindedly flicking away a speck of sand from his glass dome while diving deep among a pack of sharks – and getting his hand instantly sucked inside when the dome suddenly and unexpectedly imploded, flooding the housing and deeply cutting his wrist on the shards of broken glass. We are not implying such risks are involved with all glass domes of course – but glass breaks easily, after all, while lexan doesn't. Critics of polycarbonate lens domes will also tell you that they yellow with age, but, once more, we can only relate our own experiences – we've been using the same fish-eye dome port for twenty years and we never even noticed the slightest hint of yel-lowing. Of course you're not supposed to leave it lying under the sun for hours on end – but that obviously goes for any other piece of underwater photography equipment, including housings and strobes: always cover your rig with a clean beach towel when you're stranded waiting on the jetty or on the dive boat, not only to avoid superficial

A fairy tale, upside-down starry sky - sea stars dotting the sandy bottom in less than two meters of water at Kapalai in Malaysian Borneo. Fish-eyes can often produce spectacular images when used creatively: here the strobes' light was aimed at the closest sea star, hoping to create a colorful point of interest in an otherwise rather bland and colorless panorama bathed in mediocre visibility. High in the sky above, the sun projects the author's shadow on the sand bottom in the right lower corner - a normally serious mistake which in this case goes luckily unnoticed by most viewers.

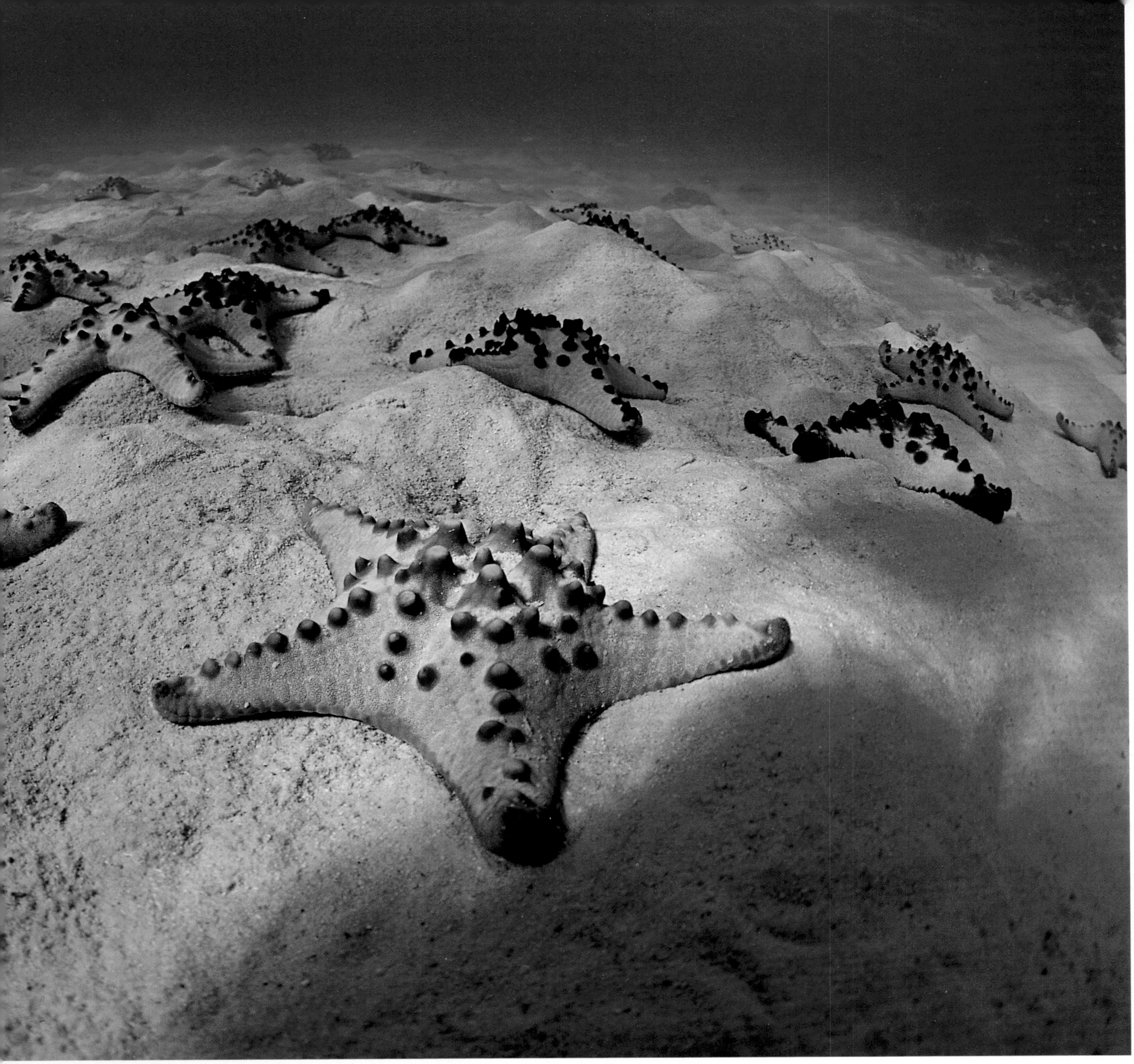

Guest
Photographer

Claudia
PELLARINI-JOUBERT
South Africa

Nikon D2X
Nikon 10.5mm fish-eye
Seacam housing
Sea & Sea YS120 dual strobes

Circling just below the surface in crystal-clear visibility, clearly set against the bright white sandy bottom below, two Caribbean reef sharks *Carcharhinus perezi* brashly contradict the all-too familiar image of lurking, imminent danger thanks to the Bahamas' sun-splashed colors and Claudia's clever use of her 10.5mm fish-eye. Dynamically opposed, their dark bronze backs lit by a network of shards of broken light mirrored from the surface above, they glide in a technicolored merry-go-round, the school of Yellowtail snappers *Ocyurus chrysurus* swimming in the opposite direction creating a startling, sunlit contrast.

damage but also – more importantly – to avoid the building up of high temperatures inside o-ring sealed equipment, such as housings or strobes, which might easily lead to flooding when entering the water.

Wide-angle lenses will provide satisfying results with large animals (including humans!) and as such are the choice of the day when diving with models (a practice we are not really interested in), mantas, pods of dolphins, medium-sized sharks, schools of barracudas or jacks and the like – even huge creatures such as whale sharks and sperm or humpback whales (if you're lucky enough to dive with them) will give much better results when portrayed using a 20mm lens rather than a fish-eye, despite what one

What at first look simply appears to be a reef panoramic shot suddenly reveals - unexpectedly mirroring the backlit shape of Antonella, swimming right above it- a large Wobbegong *Eucrossorhinus dasypogon* lurking among the corals, beautifully camouflaged on the sea bottom at Sardines, Raja Ampat, West Papua. Notice however how the attempt at lighting it evenly was not completely successful.

might instinctively think, as extreme fish-eyes tend to greatly shrink the size of any subjects not immediately adjacent while grotesquely deform those you're really getting close to. So, as a rule of thumb, if you're interested in giving a balanced, strobe-lit, naturalistic look to your large-ish subject without too much concern for the surrounding panorama, stick to a wide-angle in the 20mm range and you cannot go wrong. At the same time this is their greatest weakness, as their ease of use is counterbalanced by a certain lack of personality, so to speak. Sooner or later you'll want to stretch your creative limits, and will fall under the spell of fish-eyes – which are more difficult to use, very expensive (taking in consideration the requirement of a cumbersome dedicated dome port) and incredibly more satisfying.

Once more in the stupendously rich waters of West Papua, this time Antonella plays a more discreet counterpoint to a Coral cod *Cephalopholis miniata* emerging from an explosion of brightly colored soft corals. This image - albeit striking - might probably benefit by some judicious cropping in its lowest part, where the soft corals are both slightly out of focus and overlit.

The use of fish-eyes (10.5mm for digital, equivalent to the 16mm of film cameras) will offer you the opportunity to achieve spectacular results – once you'll have learned to manage the peculiar quirks of these short, stubby lenses. First of all, always remember that given their peculiar optical qualities, fish-eyes will greatly curve horizontal lines, increasingly so as you get away from the absolute horizontal: simply put, the more you aim up or down in relation to the horizontal, the more deformed your horizon will be. This may be fine if you are aiming for purposely deformed shots, but if you're trying instead to achieve a naturalistic image you'll always have to extremely careful with your framing, i.e. you'll have to ensure that your lens is perfectly perpendicular to your subject. On dry land, this would mean having the horizon line exactly splitting the two halves of your viewfinder, smack in the middle. Another tricky aspect of fish-eye lenses is their ability to allow panoramic, 180° fields of view – just wonderful for reef scenery or big wrecks, as long as you constantly remember that all subjects along the periphery of the image, especially close ones, will be greatly deformed: so don't put your buddy in a corner of the frame as you would do with a normal wide-angle shot and expect him to appear normal. This exceptionally wide field of view also presents a new set of problems regarding the presence of strobes and lighting in general,

A successful set-up, once again at Sardines in Raja Ampat, West Papua. Swimming in a raging current, Antonella succeeds in positioning herself at exactly the right spot above and in the background, while a slow, careful, cautious approach allows the cumbersome 16mm fish-eye dome to literally brush against the big Tasselled wobbegong *Eucrossorhynos dasypogon* lying on the sand - without spooking it and without provoking a bite! The twin strobes, spread apart and behind the camera as much as possible, light the alert but static carpet shark evenly, revealing its beautiful rosetted livery.

Guest
Photographer

Eric
CHENG

USA

Canon 1D MkII
Canon 16-35mm
Seacam housing
Ikelite DS125 dual strobes

"Jellyfish Lake" in Palau - and a few other similar locations in South East Asia - offer the opportunity to snorkel in brackish or even fresh-water secluded lakes or lagoons, mostly populated by enormous amounts of highly specialized jellyfish which have lost the capability to inflict stings. Cleverly taking advantage of a rare day of good-visibility in an otherwise normally murky habitat, Eric Cheng adds a welcome human dimension to this serene, otherworldy scene - a backlit, snorkelling girl elegantly floating among rolling, tumbling, drifting spun-sugar aliens from another world and another time.

since strobe arms and flash heads will have to be literally pulled back as much as possible to avoid entering the frame or flooding the image with unwelcome light. When working with fish-eyes it is a very good idea to have a dive buddy occasionally checking the correct positioning of your strobe heads and always remind yourself to check if they accidentally haven't entered your viewfinder's field of view. We also like to use one or two diffusers mounted on our strobe heads to achieve a softer, more natural-looking lighting when using these lenses. Since fish-eyes allow the framing of huge expanses of reefs or enormous sections of wrecks, one cannot expect to light up the whole scenery just by the use of two strobes, so natural ambient light will have to be carefully worked in

Framing what certainly is the biggest *Dendronephtya* soft coral colony we have ever encountered - as big as a human being - at Barracuda Point in Sipadan, Borneo, the best option was to take advantage of the good visibility of the day and position Antonella as far as reasonably possible - dwarfed in the distance to further add to the size and weight of such a gigantic specimen.

as part of the whole lighting of the scene. This can be achieved by switching to manual or — in several cases, especially when the background is strongly-lit blue open water — simply relying on TTL, using the strobes' flash to light up the colourful foreground and letting ambient light fill-in the background. Not really difficult, in fact, but expect to do some experimenting before finally finding the settings you're comfortable with. Another solution — made easier nowadays by the relatively higher ISO sensitivity at low noise levels offered by digital cameras than the equivalent of film — is switching the strobes off altogether and simply relying on ambient light alone to obtain atmospheric results. This involves an obvious monochromatic dominance (which can be

A more sedate and conventional image with an average-sized soft coral colony at the same location. This colorful shot demonstrates what the right proportions between the subject (in the foreground) and the human complement (in the background) should usually be in a pleasantly balanced image. Both shots taken with a 16mm fish-eye at f.11.

avoided however at shallow depths by the use of special add-ons such as Magic Filters). The amount of ambient light registered by fish-eye lenses is obviously proportional to their ample field of view, offering the possibility of reasonably small apertures (from f.8 to f.16 at 100 ASA) which, at shallow depth, will allow a wonderful depth of field even without having to resort to the use of strobes: simply put, everything in your frame will be in focus, from a few inches off your dome port to the areas stretching away in the distance. When I say "inches" or "centimeters" I mean it – being able to frame a huge stretch of reef means that everything gets shrunk in size, so to have a slightly offset focal point in your image – which you positively need to attract interest – you will have to get really close to it, almost to the point of actually touching it with your dome port (and scratching it on the corals!). This, for example, works wonders with large soft coral colonies, large gorgonian fans or even stationary, sleeping turtles in the foreground as main subjects. Remember always, the first and foremost mistake by inexperienced underwater photographers starting to use fish-eyes is shooting from too far a distance, as these lenses can be tricky for the uninitiated. So get close to your subject, and then get even closer – maintain that "fighter pilot frame of mind" mentioned in a previous chapter, hold on to your nerves, aim carefully, take your time composing your shot - and don't shoot till you see the white of their eyes!

Not all fish-eye images necessarily always need a human counterpoint or complement in the background - this exceptionally colorful reef panorama taken at Sardines in Raja Ampat, West Papua, is beautifully reminiscent of French impressionist paintings with its riot of shades and shapes, gradually fading from the violent statement in the foreground to the more subtle nuances in the distance. Notice however how the gracefully curving school of jacks in the background subtly, almost subliminally, contributes to the balance of the general image. Such wonderful shots require vibrant, pristine coral reefs and exceptional visibility - a combination not as common as one would expect.

Guest
Photographer

Alex
MUSTARD

United Kingdom

Nikon D2X
Nikon 10.5mm fish-eye
Subal housing
Subtronic Alpha dual strobes

A striking face-on Common lionfish *Pterois volitans* portrait by Alex Mustard which single-handedly rejuvenates one the most commonly photographed (and abused) fishes of the coral reef. A 10.5mm fish-eye, the big dome actually touching the subject's snout - which, understand-ably alarmed, gloriously spreads his venomous pectoral fins - with the late afternoon sun low above the surface, perfectly positioned in the background, rays of light slanting from behind the Red Sea's craggy reef coral towers. Once again, a fitting example of how a novel approach and the willingness to go against the grain - here a fish-eye is used not for a panorama but almost as a macro lens instead - will often result in highly interesting, unconventional images.

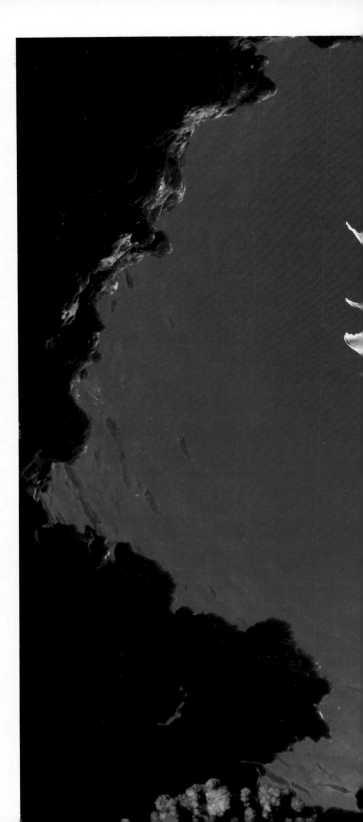

Composition is of paramount importance when dealing with fish-eyes, since there are so many different elements to be gracefully combined in the frame, and wide-angle underwater photography in general needs careful, relaxed thinking before committing to the shutter lever. Try to achieve a pleasant distribution of masses and patterns, avoiding straight horizontal or vertical lines and going for an "Expressionist" look (see Chapter 3 on Framing and Lighting for an in-depth discussion on these aspects). We are generally not interested in adding an human element to our images, as we are convinced nature is beautiful as it is and doesn't need any enhancement, but many people do, and fish-eye photography is a good opportunity to make good use of a model: a simple silhouetted

A small school of Ribbon sweetlips *Plectorhyncus polytaenia* huddles behind a coral outcrop in a raging current at Cape Kri, Raja Ampat, West Papua. The ample view and the great depth of field offered by fish-eyes can be used to advantage when shooting in less-than-friendly conditions, as in strong currents.

diver in the background will balance the general composition and add a general size comparison which is often needed in fish-eye shots to enable viewers to relate to the subject. The trick here is to keep the human element as discreet as possible, leaving the centre stage to the sophisticated elegance of nature: avoid half-naked, gauze-wrapped girl models, gaudy wetsuits, "humorous" dive hoods, wrong colour coordination or clumsy poses – these pitfalls can turn a beautiful image into a ridiculous, vulgar patchwork. Despite being clearly appreciative of nature's beauty, many underwater photographers can often also – rather strangely, in fact - display appalling bad taste in their choice of subjects. Of course you might also simply want to have a ball – so go ahead, have fun and ignore the above.

A dark underwater tunnel leading to a saltwater jungle pool is inhabited by strange sponges - mysterious, otherworldy shapes guarding the mystique of the fabled Passage in Raja Ampat, West Papua. Notice how the sun's rays stream from the forest canopy above, clearly visible beyond the water's surface thanks to the optical phenomenon known as Snell's window.

Guest
Photographer

Eric
CHENG

USA

Canon 1D MkII
Canon 15mm fish-eye
Seacam housing
Ikelite DS125 dual strobes

Completely surrounded by a rodeo of circling Grey reef sharks *Carcharhinus amblyrhynchos*, a lone diver is dwarfed by the sheer numbers of the sleek predators and the immense size of the veritable arena he finds himself in - the south pass of Fakarava in the Tuamotus of French Polynesia. All the elements of the image faultlessy click in - the elegance of the sharks, their amazing numbers, the isolation of the divers - thanks to Eric Cheng's clean ambient light shot, in which the twin strobes' flash goes almost unnoticed in the bright blue ghostliness of the oceanic seascape.

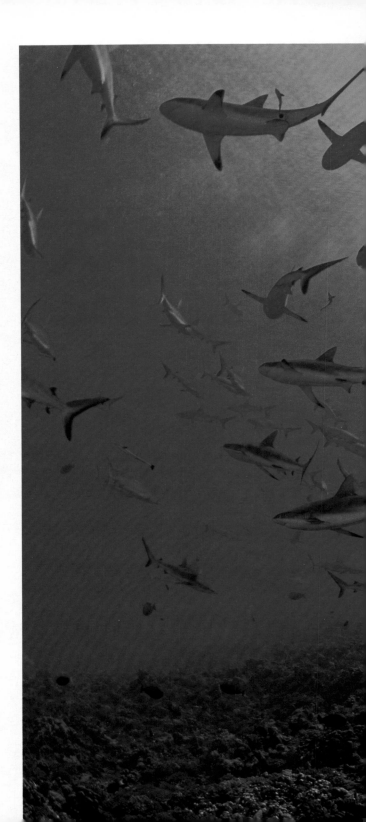

Only properly used fish-eyes can attempt to capture the magic, mystical atmosphere of The Passage, a fabled fjord-like dive site in Raja Ampat, West Papua, in which the sea and the forest intermingle. Huge gorgonians growing in shallow water, the rainforest canopy above, archerfish floating as if suspended between two worlds - correctly mixing ambient light and strobes output here is quite difficult, but the results can be truly unique and highly spectacular. Digital cameras offer quite a few advantages in such demanding conditions, allowing a much higher number of shots and being much less sensitive to suspended particles than film.

Another big favourite of underwater photographers are wrecks. We're not particularly keen on these, save the occasional WWII semi-intact plane or warship, which can still offer immediately recognizable features despite the ravages of time and warfare. However, many people are diving on them to enjoy the amount of fish life commonly found around these artificial reef systems and the encrusting organisms which cover them, and to witness the ocean slowly reclaim the work of man. Wrecks are obviously fully-fledged fish-eye domain, particularly for higher-ISO digital cameras, which allow working from a distance to fully frame the structure (or very large parts of it) with ambient light alone. Once more, a human element in the distance will be extremely useful in balancing the shot and allowing the viewer to get a sense of proportion otherwise lost, some wrecks being quite massive. Wreck photography – as with much of fish-eye work in general – needs excellent visibility to guarantee satisfying results when using strobes to enhance lighting, as the flash might otherwise generate backscatter (the undesired lighting of suspended particles in the water which causes a "snowflake" effect). When visibility is less than perfect, simply switching off the strobes and relying on ambient light alone will save the day – another of the many benefits of fish-eye lenses.

Noticed for their exceptionally intense coloration, a pair of anemones whipped by the current at shallow depth in the Maldives boldly articulate an uncompromising statement in color, texture and shape when photographed up-close with a 16mm fish-eye and strong lateral artificial lighting. The single clownfish peeking from his hide-out between the two adds a bright, contrasting note. When used in the right conditions, TTL technology allows faultless blending of ambient and artificial light.

Ketrick
CHIN
Malaysia

Nikon D2X
Nikon 10.5mm fish-eye
Nexus housing
Inon Z220S dual strobes

Pure underwater bliss - the colorful, peaceful, vibrant reef at the world-famous drop-off of Pulau Sipadan in Malaysian Borneo. Careful framing and good use of available ambient light by Ketrick Chin reinforce the serenity of this shallow-water, brightly sunlit panorama - notice how the Green turtle in the foreground has been wisely offset and how digital technology affects the image, typically reducing contrast while generating a more diffused, naturalistic lighting. Undeniably less dramatic and atmospheric than film, correctly exposed digital images are however basically more faithful to the real appearance of the underwater world as seen by scuba divers.

Guest
Photographer

Rinie
LUYKX

The Netherlands

Canon EOS 5D
Canon 17-40mm
Seacam housing
Subtronic Maxi 1 strobe

Hovering in the dark, cold, green waters of the Zeelandbrug in the Dutch Oosterschelde, two mating common cuttlefish *Sepia officinalis* flash mysterious, loving signals to each other, alien spaceships floating in a freezing somber wasteland, the only other sign of life the faint glimmer of a diver's light in the distance. Once more finding mystery and beauty in this barren world bathed in a perennial twilight, Rinie uses his zoom lens - here set at 17mm - to present us with a precious, tender peek into the private life of some of the sea's most interesting, intelligent and oft-maligned creatures. On the technical side, note how the clever use of masses and contrasting perspectives contributes to the perfect balance of the final image.

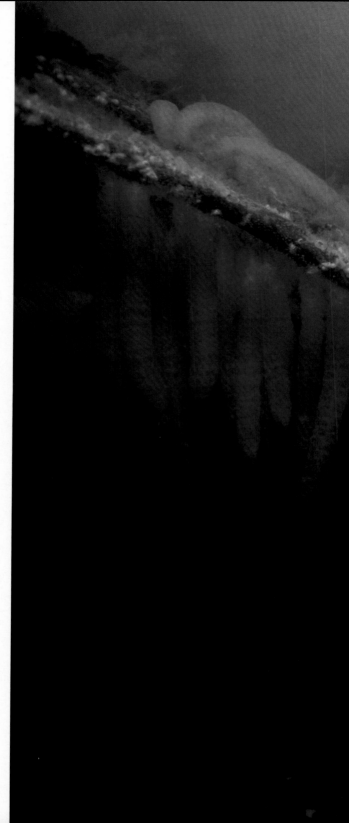

Another wonderful possibility offered by fish-eyes is the chance of getting split (also known as *half-and-half* or *over/under*) shots. These incredibly atmospheric (and very professional-looking) images are taken at water level with the upper half portraying dry land, and the lower one its underwater equivalent. Such attempts are best undertaken when both halves are simply stunning – for example, a beautiful, jungle-clad beach above, with a vibrant, untouched reef at shallow depth below. Again, the use of a snorkelling or diving model in the lower part of the frame (in the sorry absence of obliging sharks, dugongs or saltwater crocodiles!) will help in balancing the shot. Other interesting opportunities are offered by boats above and divers or large animals below, or by

Soaring above an exquisite palette of pink and orange gorgonians and untouched table corals at Mike's Point in Raja Ampat, West Papua, Antonella finds herself gliding inside a veritable Impressionist painting come alive, the green tree canopies above clearly visible through the water surface.

mixed habitat portrayals – the mangrove environment immediately comes to mind, with its vertical trees and roots binding together the world of air and water. Opportunities offered by split shots are literally endless, and will allow you to stretch your creativity. No special equipment is really needed. Despite the split-dioptre custom dome ports occasionally produced and offered (at high cost), a normal, good-quality fish-eye lens dome port will suffice. Try shooting at ambient light in very shallow water, exposing for the topside part but remembering that you'll need some depth of field to have both planes focused properly: we usually use our strobes to softly light up the bottom submerged part, working in TTL and setting apertures ranging from f.8 to f.16

Silhouetted in the distance, Antonella hovers above the gigantic sea fans 40 meters deep at Gorgonian Forest, Layang Layang, South China Sea. Notice how fish-eye shots - this one was chosen as the cover image for our *Malaysia Diving Guide* - allow for melodramatic, atmospheric effects.

A simple example of an average but rewarding half-and-half hand-held shot taken while floating on the surface with a 16mm fish-eye in Raja Ampat, West Papua. Much better results can result when shooting while standing on the bottom, allowing for finer surface tuning and strobe positioning. When shooting above/under it is necessary to use a high aperture setting (f.11 or f.16) to ensure both focal planes (the background above and the foreground underwater) are in focus.

Fish-eyes can also be successfully used to exaggerate perspective, as in this close-up portrayal - taken in West Papua - of a colonial anemone and its attending clownfish, probably a local yellow-tailed variation of *Amphiprion melanopus*. No other lens would have been able to capture the broad extension of the colony, which measured more than three meters in width and which numbered at least twenty adult anemonefish occupants. Quite a sight - startingly captured by vertically positioning the fish-eye just a few centimeters off the closest tentacles and shooting in TTL at a very shallow depth.

at 1/125 to have both focal planes in focus. If you elect to rely on ambient light alone, you'll be forced to resort to a longer exposure time, getting almost guaranteed blurry shots. Remember, the camera is generally floating while you, if fortunate, are standing in water up to your chest trying to keep the water line perfectly horizontal – which is not exactly easy. So you might want to consider the use of a long-legged monopod or even a tripod to steady your camera. It goes without saying that such images should only be attempted in glass-flat water, and that most of the unavoidable water drops coalescing and collecting on the upper half of your dome port, exposed to air, will have to be later removed with Photoshop. Perfect split images are not easy to achieve as many factors beyond one's control have to click together – but when they do, the results can truly be exciting.

Fish-eye heaven - the incredibly rich and colorful coral reefs of Raja Ampat in West Papua, often blessed with optimal visibility but equally often scourged by raging currents. Such spectacular underwater vistas and such challenging conditions call for daily use of wide-angle and fish-eye lenses - ideally suited for touch-and-go shooting, when there is little time for fine tuning and one has to rely heavily on one-hand photography and instinctive composition.

Chapter 8

TOPSIDE TRAINING
We all do dive intervals, don't we?

- Who needs these?
- Practice your skills
- Why you need a good model
- Spare camera, extra lenses, waterproof bag

I yet have to encounter an underwater photographer who doesn't secretly or not-so-secretly cultivate the dream of seeing his or her own photographs finally published. As if the act of committing the image to paper would somehow imbue it with a touch of immortality, a sprinkle of eternity – or, more simply, make it more dignified in the eyes of others. Ah, the admiration of peers, the envy of less-capable (or less-interested, presumably) fellow divers, the deceiving red carpet of celebrity! Now, we all have to honestly admit very little of this actually takes place in the real world, since not many underwater shutterbugs can boast of writing skills to match their photographic ones. If you really want to commercially publish in serious magazines and books, good pictures without an equally engaging text are of little value. The

Strolling on a deserted beach on Walea island in Northern Sulawesi, Antonella chances upon a beached *Nautilus* shell - an interesting visual opportunity which allows us to stray from the usual postcard-like tropical beach shot we all see much too often. A circular polarizer kills some of the glare while bringing out the majestic cloud formations in the background. Wide-angle lenses are generally preferable to fish-eyes for panoramic topside shots, providing a more balanced, easily-related to image and avoiding the curved horizons and deformed corners of the latter.

The idyllic panorama from Sorido Bay Resort's wooden jetty in Raja Ampat, West Papua - not a soul in sight and a good example of the difficulties inherent in the topside use of fish-eyes. Great care was taken to keep the horizon perfectly level, but nothing could be done to avoid the deformed corners typical of such lenses. Despite their quirks, fish-eyes can often provide dramatic results in topside photography - especially when the human element is simply used as an offset element and the main focus is on the landscape. Notice the splash of color added by the bright yellow fins.

market is also small, and competition fierce. However, what really surprises us no end is how those same obsessed divers, who will spend long exhausting hours underwater trying to get that elusive "perfect" shot, will carelessly put their camera aside once on dry land again, forgetting it till the next dive and simply ignoring the beauty of the surrounding landscape and the numerous photo opportunities that dive intervals commonly offer. Now, we all have to remember that even the most highly specialized dive magazine will be seriously in need of a few descriptive topside shots and, after you have hopefully graduated to mainstream travel periodicals, those will simply become mandatory.

Landscape and people shots are basically needed by magazine editors to help their mainstream public relate more easily to the subject of the article – not all readers are hardcore divers, remember. The most interesting aspects of the place you're visiting should always be a top priority, at least if you are serious about putting a decent reporting package together. So concentrate on documenting the surrounding environment, the customs of local people, and the pre-dive activity – be this on land or on a boat. Simple basics include colourful examples of local flora and fauna (editors like close-ups, even if they have been conveniently taken in a nearby zoo – you might want to turn a blind eye on this and accept a little cheating here), clear images of the resort you're staying at – including your hopefully uncluttered room and the

Antonella snorkelling on Kri island's house reef in Raja Ampat, West Papua - here the typical curvature of the horizon generated by fish-eyes when not kept perfectly level is used to reinforce the feeling of quiet remoteness of this pristine location. With the benefit of hindsight, a more colorful, color-coordinated set of bikinis and fins would have probably been preferable - black looks a bit too severe in such a brightly lit, paradisiacal setting.

Guest
Photographer

Leon
JOUBERT
South Africa

Nikon Coolpix 5200

An absolutely brilliant, intuitive and very commercial shot which would make a wonderful travel magazine article double-spread - Leon Joubert was quick to realize the potential of the set up when he passed by these beach chairs in the Bahamas, a splash of merry candy colors against the jade green of the brightly sunlit ocean in the background. It all came together in a few seconds - his wife Claudia taking a seat, a speedboat racing in from the side, barely enough time to frame and shoot almost by reflex. The results are simple but perfectly balanced and quite pleasant. Fumbling with the controls of a more complex DSLR rather than relying on the simple point-and-shoot employed here would have probably resulted in missing the shot.

surrounding facilities (think of jetties, swimming pools, restaurants, anchored dive boats, pre-dive briefings) and an ample coverage of the most scenic spots in the neighbourhood. This may appear obvious, but you'd be surprised by how unimaginative magazine editors (and their readers) can be. Bright turquoise swimming pools with attendant colourful, flower-decorated cocktail glasses, exotic vegetation in bloom, cute close-ups of smiling local kids, flaming tropical sunsets and a pretty model on a deserted beach can still work wonders. Some things will never change! I know it sounds trite, but it's true nonetheless – and to be completely honest, not everybody can take such pictures anyway. Taking commercially viable shots is an art by itself and a perfectly respectable one even if we don't want to talk too deeply about it here. However, think of it as a good opportunity to hone your skills and as a required supplement to your beautiful underwater shots. Again, it will require some discipline and a willingness to work and experiment (most often when your fellow divers will be snoring away or simply relaxing), but practising topside photography on a regular basis will help in picking up novel ideas which might come in handy underwater, build up confidence in your model

A tame White pelican *Pelecanus onocrotalus* encountered on Madoogali island's beach in the Maldives archipelago immediately called for a fisheye shot, its bright white plumage and huge beak offering a beautiful counterpoint to the flat, peaceful expanse of the Indian Ocean in the late afternoon. Great care was obviously taken in keeping the horizon perfectly level and corner deformation minimized - such an arresting image needs no distracting elements.

(if you are working with one on a regular basis) and refine your style. There's an incredible difference between a just-for-fun snapshot mindlessly taken at a breakfast table and a professionally arranged image of the same situation. You don't need to be a full-time professional to do it – it just takes some creativity and a little imagination: take a good, hard look at the arresting images you can find on most travel magazines and do your best to emulate them. By checking a few, you'll soon be able to notice constantly recurring themes and technical solutions you can easily and consciously imitate. Later on, when you'll be more confident, you'll be able to develop your own style. The general idea is to achieve a certain elegance, using the human element to discreetly accent the natural beauty of the surroundings. Not really difficult when you're travelling in the tropics, surrounded by some of the world's most beautiful scenery. Again, these are simple truths, but a throwaway click at your sun-burnt partner slouched half-asleep in a sundeck chair won't be of any use, not even as a good souvenir of your holiday. Always try to consciously achieve good poses instead, thinking of possible later editorial needs: as a simple example, try offsetting your model to the right or to the left, leaving enough

The use of natural props - here a conveniently located outrigger canoe on Wai island's beach in Raja Ampat, West Papua - often results in engaging, very natural-looking images. Avoiding contrived, pseudo-humorous or ungraceful poses is of paramount importance in these occasions - having the model look directly away from the camera is a seldom-used but very useful little visual trick to bring the viewer's attention to the actual surrounding panorama.

Wading in knee-deep water at sunset in Pulau Lankayan resulted in this moving image of two Hawksbill turtle *Eretmochelys imbricata* hatchlings, almost huddling together while taking the first swim of their life - the strobe's flash freezing their paddling towards an uncertain future. The 16mm fish-eye was literally framing them at water level.

A wooden rack covered with fish drying in the sun, the clear water behind, a dramatic cloud formation in the background above the jungle-clad inhabited islands of Raja Ampat, West Papua. Simple but atmospheric, this image exemplifies well the typically easy and yet too often overlooked opportunity encountered by divers in the tropics.

room in the finished image so that a title and a summary for the travel article can be added by the magazine staff. I have been a professional, full-time magazine chief-of-staff for the past thirty years, and you cannot imagine the amount of good pictures I've seen going unused because our layout designer couldn't find enough room to stick a title and a summary on them. Also remember that really good photographs could end up as double-page spreads, so having the main subject slightly offset to either side will solve the problem of centre folding – the bane of photo editors. Such simple advice works perfectly fine underwater too, as we have seen in the previous chapters, so quickly teach yourself the basic routine of framing, focusing on your subject, re-composing and shooting till it becomes second nature. Fellow divers or obliging travel companions do not actually need to be professional models as long as they have a reasonably trim figure, a graceful posture and above all a good-humoured willingness to "pose" for you with a vengeance, acting like they were the real deal. It can be great fun, and if you both take it with just a little pinch of determination you won't only greatly enjoy yourself – the chances are you'll get some pretty good shots too. You'll be surprised! Before packing for a dive trip think of this possibility and act accordingly – bright, day-glo colours and pretty swim gear can make or break a beach photograph if you decide to have a model in it, bare feet will always be better than worn-out, ugly sandals, sun-tanned will do while fish-belly white won't, and wearing

A juvenile Blacktip shark *Carcharhinus melanopterus* hunts for crabs and small fish in ankle-deep water by the beach of Pulau Lankayan at dawn. Photographers interested in local topside fauna will necessarily have to wander alone and in the very early morning - the best time of the day for forest birds and beach-dwelling species.

Mangrove habitats - when not inhabited by dangerous species such as
Saltwater crocodiles - offer an incredible array of photographic
opportunities to the adventurous. This interesting shot - which might
almost qualify as a split image - was taken in West Papua while wading in
chin-deep water, pointing the 10.5mm fish-eye towards the surface and
keeping the housing and its dome just under the surface:
in the resulting dizzying image it is almost impossible to discern where
water ends and air begins, a perfect photographic depiction of the finely
balanced mangrove universe.

340

The often-seen and much-abused "postcard shot" from the beach at the tropics - obvious maybe, but not necessarily easy. Good light conditions, dramatic cloud formations, a beautiful general environment and - most importantly - a good model able to pose naturally are an absolute must. It often takes several attempts to achieve the right pose - it can be highly enjoyable and pleasant fun, but it also has to be taken very seriously if the results have to stand out from the crowd. Most travel magazines will be highly interested in good images of this kind - much more than in underwater ones, in fact.

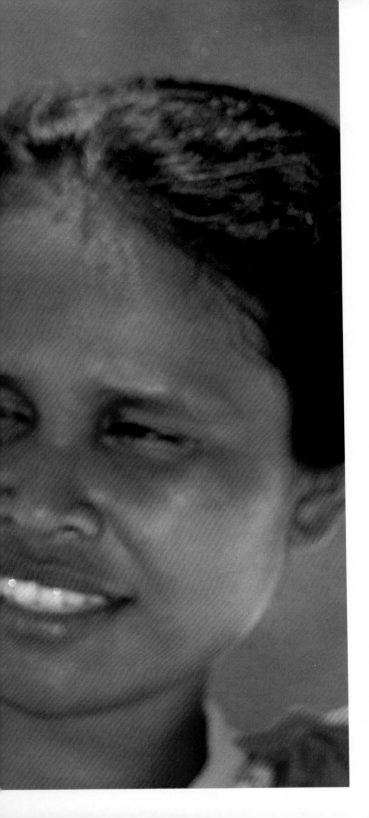

snazzy reflective sunglasses will always be better than grimacing horri-
bly while squinting at the tropical sun. And if you're really going to be
serious about this, always have your models sign you a release document for future use of the images in which they appear – you don't
want to be sued by somebody you met only once because your lucky
shot has been used in a worldwide advertising campaign without his or
her consent.

Another opportunity you cannot afford missing whenever you have a
chance is aerial shooting. Few people in the publishing and advertising
business will resist the shimmering allure of a beautiful tropical atoll as
seen from the sky, so always try to secure window-seats with unob-
structed views when island-hopping on the wing and, above all, try to
fly by helicopter whenever possible, since these wonderful contrap-
tions often sport opening side windows. Wide-angle lenses and polar-
izing filters will come in handy when shooting from the air, and always
remember to use high shutter speeds (1/125 and faster) to avoid blur-
ring – you won't need a lot of depth of field, so an aperture of f.5.6 at
ISO 100 will suffice most of the time. Since we are on the subject of
camera equipment, we should stress another aspect of topside dive
travel which is a bit less obvious than the previous ones and that is the
utmost importance of always carrying along a spare camera body.
Lugging another camera body, a second housing and two more extra

Letting somebody else do the modelling for once, Antonella was able to shoot this
tender image of a local baby and his proud mommy during a dive interval spent on Wai
island beach in Raja Ampat, West Papua. People portraits are best taken from a distance
with a good zoom lens to avoid openly interfering with their natural expressions - for
heavily-laden, air-travelling scuba divers the revolutionary, small and exceptionally light
Nikon 18-200mm has proven a true blessing. Similar images of a very high quality can
also be successfully taken with very small, zooming point-and-shoots.

Guest
Photographer

Will CHEN
USA

Canon 5D
Canon 16-35mm
Ikelite housing
Ikelite DS125 strobe

The business end of a Lemon shark *Negaprion brevirostris* breaches the calm surface of the Bahamas' waters, proving an irresistible temptation for Will Chen's 16-35mm zoom. Look at those teeth! Despite what one might be tempted to think at first sight, this stunning image was actually shot from the dive boat's swimstep, hand-holding and lowering the housed camera in the water after having pre-set the focus at about 30 centimeters and having locked it. The single strobe used for fill-in and the high shutter speed employed - 1/200 of a second - froze the action with dramatic results.

strobes along might be stretching it a bit too much (we did, for twenty years, just to be on the safe side – but again, we were both taking
pictures underwater), but taking a spare, identical body of the same
camera brand and model is an absolute necessity. Not only because
your main body might unexpectedly malfunction or even get flooded
(even though it is not supposed to happen), but mostly because in this
way you'll always have a second, fully lens-compatible, working camera
system at hand without having to open and more or less dismantle
your precious underwater housing every time you want to take a fleeting topside picture. Opening your fully latched and properly set-up
housing to hurriedly take your camera out, frantically changing the lens
amidst saltwater spray and fixing everything up again in the hope of
catching a good shot of those frolicking dolphins on your way to the
dive site is a sure recipe for disaster. Too many things can go wrong –
sand or a hair can stick to your o-rings, the camera can fall from your
slippery wet fingers, the strobe connection can be badly pulled, the
housing can be latched improperly and flood – you see the general picture. Always having a spare camera body and a couple of lenses ready
will save you a lot of headaches and disappointments, allowing you to
safely shoot fellow divers entering the water and big marine life on the
surface, not to mention the surrounding landscape and the occasional
once-in-a-lifetime, deserted island beach panorama. It's worth carrying
everything in a small, water-proof, well-padded camera bag you can

Good aerial shots usually prove invaluable in publishing - when selling feature articles
to travel and/or dive magazines, or when publishing books like this one. Very few people
can resist the visual allure of a tropical atoll sitting in a turquoise sea - like this one
from the Maldives archipelago. Always try to shoot from opening windows - occasionally
available on single-engine tourist planes - employing wide-angles and high
shutter speeds (at least 1/250) to avoid engine vibration and blurred images.
Depth of field is not important at these heights - f.4 or f.5.6 will do nicely.

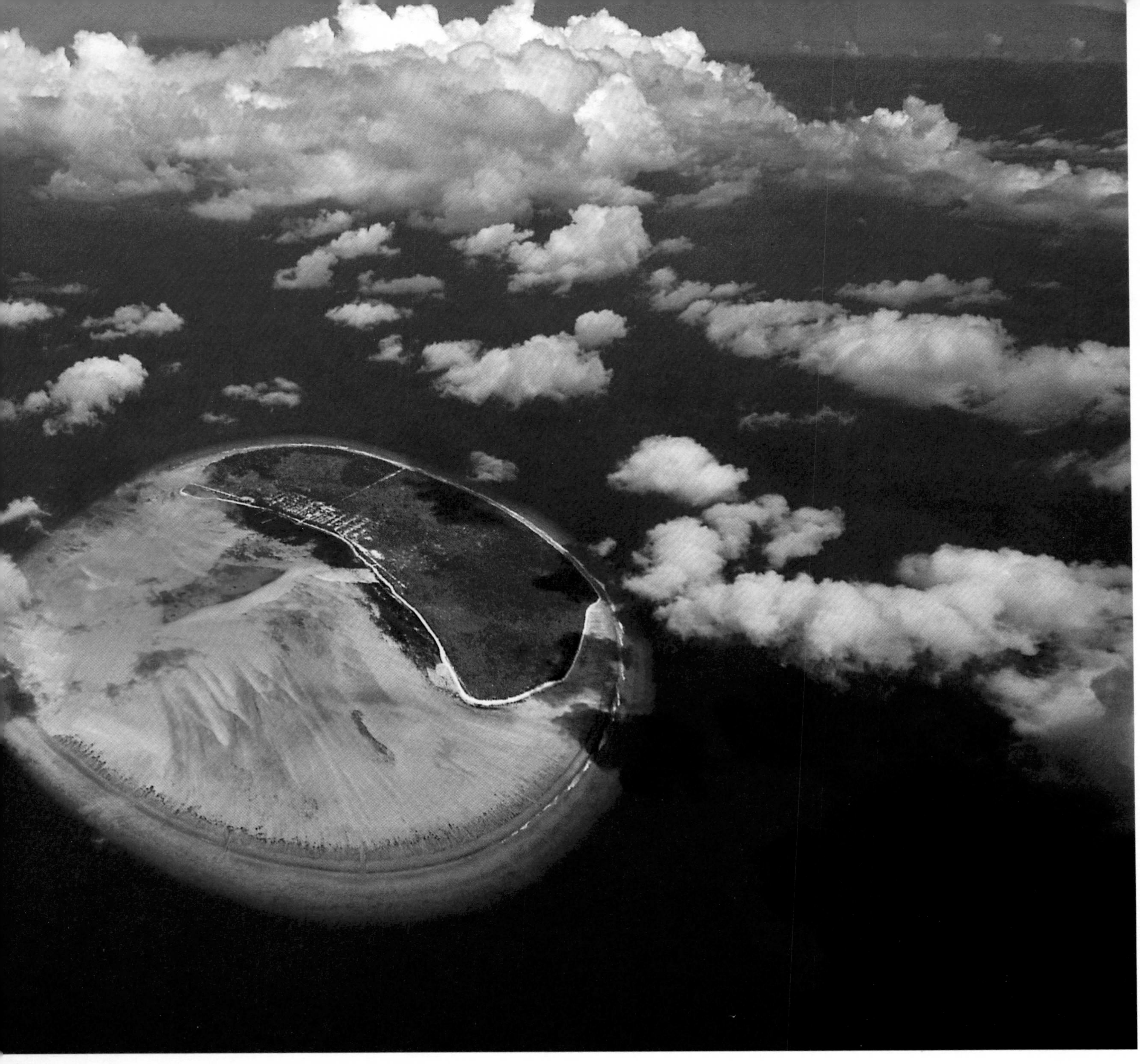

Helicopter photography is the absolute best in aerial shooting - this striking image of Pulau Lankayan and its attending coral reefs was taken while freely standing outside in the open air on the pontoon of a rented helicopter. Shooting in these exhilarating but demanding conditions requires the mandatory use of a strongly buckled safety lanyard and firm hands - one doesn't want to have an expensive wide-angle lens or camera body slip away and take a dip here!

Guest
Photographer

Alberto Luca
RECCHI

Italy

Nikon F4
Nikon 80-200mm

This is no chance shot - rather, the spectacular result of long tiring hours spent scanning the surface from the rocking safety of a boat's broadside, anxiously waiting for that split-second opportunity which will only present itself once in a lifetime. Alberto has succeeded in freezing the action at its dynamic best, the enormous bulk of the Great white shark *Carcharodon carcharias* at the apex of its vaulting killer jump, the body of its sea lion prey literally disappearing in its cavernous jaws. I'm not really sure I'd like to see this during one of my dive intervals!

Tony WU

Japan

Canon 1D MkII
Canon 100-400mm

It would be too obvious and easy captioning this image with something sounding like "waving good-bye" - Tony Wu's moving and arresting shot of a Humpback whale's vertically raised pectoral fin at sunset strikes in fact a deeper chord. Almost abstract in its rugged simplicity, it is a living monument and testimonial to the power and grace of these beautiful creatures - and a great example of marine photography taken from a boat.

safely tuck away somewhere in the dive boat, ready to be rapidly pulled out but well away from clumsy fellow divers, rolling empty tanks and dangerous saltwater spray. Get one with a small shoulder strap or even a small back-pack, so you'll be able to easily take it along with you should the opportunity to visit some small island or local fishing village present itself. One good-for-all lens like the wonderful Nikon 18-200mm zoom will generally cover most subjects, from jumping dolphins to models posing on the beach and beaming village kids, but do not forget taking a polarizer along as strong light reflection on white sand tropical beaches can be a real pain to deal with, even if digital technology can today handle that much better than film. Small point-and-shoot digital cameras, today almost always equipped with sophisticated, powerful zoom lenses and roomy memory cards, can also repre-sent the ideal choice regarding land photography when on a dive trip, but do not expect (yet!) to have the same con-trol and flexibility offered by a DSLR, which is still our tool of choice at the time of writing. Of course this entails work and more work (not to mention extra hassles and costs), and the actual risk of taking all the fun away from your hard-earned holidays will get more and more consis-

Sunset turns the Sulawesi Sea into a pool of liquid gold at Kapalai in Malaysian Borneo - the hour of twilight when all the elements in nature briefly meet and blend into one. Most divers will usually miss such beautiful photographic opportunities - too tired from the day's diving, or sitting in front of their laptop, too engrossed in the day's images. Nature does not wait - one has to be quick, alert and always willing to capture her fleeting magic.

Guest
Photographer

Eric
CHENG
USA

Canon 1D MkII
Canon 70-200mm

Frolicking dolphins at sunset in False Bay, Simonstown, South Africa - captured in a magic blink by Eric Cheng's camera, proving once more that zoom lenses - in this case a Canon 70-200mm - truly represent the optimal choice for dive interval and general topside shots by divers. Shooting fast-moving subjects at sea at dawn or twilight and from a moving boat can prove exceedingly difficult - sharply focused, unblurred images require high shutter speeds and full aperture. VR or vibration-reduction technology available to many new digital cameras and lenses can prove itself useful in these occasions, but results are too random to guarantee success by its use alone.

GUEST PHOTOGRAPHER

tent. However, you honestly need to take all the trouble mentioned above only if you're really, really keen on having your shots published. Then, with success, the personal satisfaction of having achieved something worthwhile will have more than compensated for the worries, costs and frustrations encountered in the process.

So again, once more, we return to our initial question: *"Why, oh, why in the world are we doing this?"* Are we simply looking for fun? Do we strive for professional results? Are we trying to achieve artistic creation? Or do we feel the urge to document a vanishing, beautiful world? Sooner or later we'll all be able to find an answer, each of us in our own way. In the meantime — let's dive!

A dramatic, fiery sunset over the coast of Sabah in Malaysian Borneo - a last, tripod-assisted effort to capture the world's beauty after a long day's diving. Cumbersome and heavy, professional tripods can often however prove absolutely invaluable in very low-light situations. Is it worth taking one along, considering the extra baggage weight and carry-on current restrictions on planes? It depends - as in so many other matters debated in this book - there is no set answer. You decide!